MW00412665

HANDBOOK OF
SPANISH-ENGLISH TRANSLATION

Lucía V. Aranda

University Press of America,® Inc.
Lanham · Boulder · New York · Toronto · Plymouth, UK

Copyright © 2007 by
University Press of America,® Inc.
4501 Forbes Boulevard
Suite 200
Lanham, Maryland 20706
UPA Acquisitions Department (301) 459-3366

Estover Road
Plymouth PL6 7PY
United Kingdom

Library of Congress Control Number: 2007922244
ISBN-13: 978-0-7618-3730-5 (clothbound : alk. paper)
ISBN-10: 0-7618-3730-2 (clothbound : alk. paper)
ISBN-13: 978-0-7618-3729-9 (paperback : alk. paper)
ISBN-10: 0-7618-3729-9 (paperback : alk. paper)

For Craig
in love and language

Table of Contents

Preface

No longer consigned exclusively to linguistics or literature, translation studies has evolved into an interdisciplinary field that bridges linguistics, literary studies, economics, history, psychology, anthropology, film and cultural studies. It is my intention with this book to introduce undergraduate students to the main theoretical and practical aspects of translation.

There are two main sections in *The Handbook of Spanish-English Translation*. In the first six chapters I have tried to document the growth of translation studies. In Chapter 1, I lay out the main issues of translation such as the meaning of equivalence and the possible text types. The eternal dilemma of whether translations should 'tend' towards the language and culture of the original or towards those of the translation is explored in the second chapter.

Chapter 3 is divided along chronological lines: the first part deals with the history of translation before the 20th century and, the second, with the development of translation studies as an increasingly significant academic field. In the fourth chapter, "*Traduttore, traditore*. Shaping Culture through Translation," I explore translation as an exercise in rewriting, as a colonial tool of linguistic imperialism and a factor in canon formations. In Chapter 5, the reader is presented with a description of the modes of interpretation (e.g. simultaneous, consecutive, community or liaison). Dubbing and subtitling as well as other audiovisual translation modes are set against the background of censorship (e.g. in Franco's Spain). The last chapter of the first part of the book is more practical in its approach for the Spanish-English contrastive analysis is intended as a tangible complement to translation as an art.

The second half of the book is composed of original texts in Spanish and English, with their published translations. Each selection is briefly introduced with information regarding the author and the text. It is said translators are invisible. I have made every attempt to give credit to the translators behind my selection of published translations; those who do not receive credit in this book is because their published translations do not recognize them for their work. I have included all the nuances of the originals and their translations, errors and all –all other mistakes are my own. Compiled as specific examples for the study of the craft of translation, a number of the texts have more than one version. The selection includes poems, excerpts from novels, a movie script, a comic strip, academic works and government documents.

It is not surprising translation studies is one of the fastest growing academic fields in the arts and humanities: from the translation of Buddhist scriptures into Chinese (1100 BC), to Cicero's translation of the Greeks (46 BC), to the *Escuela de Traductores de Toledo* (14th century), La Malinche interpreting for Moctezuma and Hernán Cortés (16th century), Martin Luther's translation of the Bible into German (1534), or machine translation, translation has played a key role in the development of world history and culture. I hope readers find the intricacies of translation presented in this *Handbook* as fascinating as they are for me.

Acknowledgements

I would like to thank the following authors and copyright holders for allowing me to reprint material for this book:

Majorie Agosín, "Cuentos de hadas y algo más" and "Fairy tales and Something More," translation by Cola Franzen. In *Brujas y algo más / Witches and Other Things*, pp. 16-17. © 1984 by Latin American Literary Review Press. Reprinted by kind permission of the author and the Latin American Literary Review Press.

David Altabe, *Symphony of Love. Las rimas by Gustavo Adolfo Bécquer*, p. 59. With kind permission of the author.

American Diabetes Association, *Could You Be at Risk for Diabetes* and *¿Podría Usted Estar a Riesgo de Tener Diabetes?* Copyright © 2006 American Diabetes Association, reprinted with permission from *The American Diabetes Association*. Call 1-800-232-6733 or order online at http://store.diabtes.org.

Guillermo Cabrera Infante, *Tres tristes tigres*, Barcelona: Seix Barral, 1998, pp. 13-14, and *Three Trapped Tigers*, translation by Donald Gardener and Suzanne Jill Levine, New York: Harper & Row, 1971, pp. 3-4. © 1967 by G. Cabrera Infante. Reprinted by kind permission from the heirs of Guillermo Cabrera Infante and Agencia Literaria Carmen Balcells, S.A.

John M. Coetzee, *Life & Times of Michael K*, London: Penguin Books, 1983, pp. 3-4 and *Vida y época de Michael K*, translations Concha Manella, Madrid: Ediciones Alfaguara, 1987, 17-18, and Barcelona: Mondadori, 2006, 9-10. Copyright by J.M. Coetzee, 1983. All rights reserved. Used by permission of the Peter Lampack Agency, Inc.

Arthur Golden. *Memoirs of a Geisha*, New York: Random House, 1997, 1-2 and *Memorias de una geisha*, translation Pilar Vázquez, 2002, 9-10. ©1997 by Arthur Golden. Used by permission of Alfred A. Knopf, a division of Random House, Inc.

Antonio Jiménez Barca, *El negocio de inventar nombres / Hallowed be thy brand name*, used by permission of © Diario El País, S.L.

Humberto López Morales, "Estructuras internas, estructuras externas y traducción" and "Deep Structure, Surface Structure and Translation," translation María Esther Castro. In *Problemas de la Traducción / Problems in Translation*, Editorial de la Universidad de Puerto Rico, pp. 12-13. ©1982 The University of Puerto Rico.

José Martí, *Versos sencillos / Simple Verses*, translation Manuel A. Tellechea. By kind permission of Arte Público Press, pp, 16-23. ©1997. *Versos sencillos. A Dual Language Edition*, translation Anne Fountain. By kind permission of Anne Fountain and McFarland & Company, Inc.

Eugene A. Nida and Charles R. Taber, *The Theory and Practice of Translation*, p. 33, Figure 6, ©1969. Used by kind permission of E. J. Brill, Leiden.

Tomás Rivera, *...y no se lo tragó la tierra* © 1971, p. 2 *...And the Earth Did Not Devour Him*, translation Evangelina Vigil-Piñon © 1995, p. 83. Used by kind permission of Arte Público Press.

Charles Schulz, *Peanuts*, ©1990, 06/18/90. Used with kind permission by © United Feature Syndicate.

Mary Snell-Hornby, *Translation Studies: An Integrated Approach*, ©1995, pg. 32. With kind permission by John Benjamins Publishing Company, Amsterdam/Philadelphia.

Henry Sullivan, *The Poems of Gustavo Adolfo Bécquer: A Metrical, Linear Translation*, 2002, p. 40. With kind permission of Joe Zdenek and Spanish Literature Publications Company.

George Yule *The Study of Language*, ©1988, pg. 18-19. *El lenguaje*, translation Nuria Bel Rafecas, ©1990 pg. 33-34. Used by kind permission of the author and Cambridge University Press.

I am indebted to many people for their inspiration, support, and expertise. First and foremost, I would like to thank Lourdes Ortega for her detailed comments, warmth and kindness. I owe a debt of gratitude to my wonderful friends and colleagues of Spanish at the University of Hawai'i. My thanks also to Patti Belcher at University Press of America for her encouragement, to Cherie Hayes-Gigante for her careful revisions and to my students, for exploring the paths of translation together. A Research Relations Fund Award from the University of Hawaii provided support for this book.

A special thanks to Amalia, Ana, Cecilia, Concha, Laura, Meme, and my parents Lucía and José Luis for their support and encouragement, without whom I would not have been able to finish this book. And last, but not least, I would like to thank Camila, Carita and Nicky for their loving patience and my husband, Craig Chaudron, for exploring ideas, and sharing his love and intelligence with me. How I wish you were still here...

Chapter 1

Issues in Translation

Translators have been referred to as writers, rewriters, authors, translator-text authors, imitators, and even technical stuntmen, and although they are able to copyright their translations in some countries, their status remains ambiguous and largely invisible in most parts of the world.[1] The debate on authorship revolves around the notion of whether a translation is a copy of an original, or an original in another language. What is an original? Writers such as Octavio Paz or Jorge Luis Borges, for example, do not consider writers originators of original ideas but appropriators of previous works. For Paz (1986):

> Each text is unique, yet at the same time it is the translation of another text. No text is entirely original, because language itself is essentially a translation. In the first place, it translates from the non-verbal world. Then, too, each sign, each sentence, is the translation of another sign, another sentence. This reasoning may even be reversed without losing any of its force and we may assert that all texts are original because every translation is different. To a certain extent every translation is an original invention and thus constitutes a unique text.

Venuti (1998, 43) expands on this issue by stating that:

> Translation can be considered a form of authorship, but an authorship now redefined as derivative, not self-originating. Authorship is not *sui generis*; writing depends on pre-existing cultural materials, selected by the author, arranged in an order of priority, and rewritten (or elaborated) according to specific values.

Clearly, translators are not value-free. The Romans substituted Greek cultural markers with Roman ones and replaced the author's name with the translator's (e.g.: Terence combined translations of Greek comedies and presented them as his own)[2]; other translators have eliminated sexual images of homosexuality or references to body parts because they thought these would 'upset' the new readers; others have altered the form of the original text and erased the literary singularity of a writer to fit the target canon (e.g. the elimination of Faulkner's stream-of-consciousness in *Absalom, Absalom!* in one Spanish version, Manella, 2000). According to reception theory, which stems from the hermeneutic notion associated with Schleiermacher and Heidegger that that language forms reality (and challenging the position that words represent images not that words represent images),[3] culture can influence a translation more than linguistic considerations. It follows then that translators will interpret the source texts based on their own values and will pass these on in the translated text; the more scientific and technical or 'valueless' the text, the less noticeable the interpretation of the translator as reader. For Popovic (1970, 70) translation includes the transference of intellectual and aesthetic qualities of the source text into the translated text.

Translation, the transfer of a message from one language into another –the oral transfer of a spoken message being interpretation– defies definition because of the multiple variants involved in the process (i.e. text translation, mathematical translation or even radio transmission translation). For Robinson (2000, 6) translation is "different things for different people. For people that are not translators, it is primarily a text; for people who are, it is primarily an activity."

It is widely assumed translators translate optimally from their native-like learned language into their strongest or native language, although in Eastern Europe the inverse is assumed. However, directionality of translation can also be determined by the situation of languages and translators at a given moment.[4] Some basic translation terminology includes:

ST   the source text or original
SL   the source language or language of the original
TT   the target text or translation
TL   the target language or the language of the translation
LA   the language a person knows best, the mother tongue in which the translator has native competency, and which s/he should translate into optimally
LB   the language in which a person has native or near-native competency, and which translators usually translate from (rarely into)
LC   the language in which a person has a passive competency, less than their LB, but enough to be able to translate from

Undoubtedly, the most tangible element of a translation, the text, from bottom-up comprises words, content, meanings, allusions, form, and function, all of which must be carefully reproduced in another language –all in all a daunting task. It follows that Benjamin (1969, 90) would compare translations to broken vases, with pieces which "must fit at every point, though none may be exactly like the other," and Sayers Peden (1989, 13) to an ice cube that melts to become an ice cube again, but different. Translators frequently must decide if they are to be faithful to the form (especially difficult if the text is a poem, is rhymed, plays on words, etc.), to its content, or to its function. But as Nida and Taber (1969, 4) affirm "Anything that can be said in one language can be said in another, unless the form is an essential element of the message." The fact that translated texts are usually longer than the original attests to the imprecision of the linguistic transference as well as to the decision-making process of translators, both of which compromise the ST and the TT. Choices are made at the macro and micro level, and involve deciding on a translation strategy for the whole text (Wilss 2004, 57-60) as well as the choice of a single word; it is thought translators often have to make more decisions than the original author at the word level. Sayers Peden's collection of 17 different versions of a poem by Sor Juana Inés de la Cruz is but one testament to exactly how much variation there can be in decision-making in translation (Sayers Peden 1989).

While translation studies now researches topics such as canon formation (e.g.: the translation of classics via translations in India) or gender issues (e.g.: the different translation strategies of women and men), or post-colonial issues (e.g.: linguistic imperialism), the issue of equivalence in translation is central to translation studies and was especially so in the 1960s and 1970s. Also referred to as fidelity, faithfulness, accuracy, sameness or correspondence, equivalence remains an ideal in translation and slippery to define. The difficulty resides in measuring the notion of equivalency. Is equivalence achieved through formal correspondence (i.e. at the linguistic level) or through functional correspondence (i.e. of the extralinguistic features)? What to do with the obligatory features of languages or the lack of lexical items or concepts? How to weigh the linguistic features against the social ones? Is equivalence achieved by producing in an audience the same effect it had on the original readers or by replicating all the details of the original even at the risk of the reader not understanding references, allusions or linguistic expressions? Is equivalence to be found by rewriting a text for a target audience who will never be able to tell he or she is reading a translation (i.e. under the illusion of transparency, Venuti 1995, 1) or is equivalence an extremely close translation of the original, so close that the reader can 'see' the original text? It is believed that where there is less interpretation possible, it is more imperative and less difficult to attain a certain degree of equivalence. However, in poetry, ads, puns, sayings, irony, or jokes, which rely on connotations, equivalence seems less attainable and labored. On the other hand, why attempt any degree of equivalency with the original? Berman, for example, eschews the notion because "to play with 'equivalence' is to attack the discourse of the foreign work" (Berman 2003, 295). In fact, is equivalence success?

The Translator's Charter, drawn up by FIT (*Fédération Internationale de Traducteurs*) and adopted by UNESCO in Nairobi in 1976 (1994, 15) states that, "Every translation shall be faithful and render exactly the idea and form of the original — this fidelity constituting both a moral and legal obligation for the translator." The next point in the Translator's Charter clarifies this idea of fidelity: "A faithful translation, however, should not be confused with a literal translation, the fidelity of a translation not excluding an adaptation to make the form, the atmosphere and deeper meaning of the work felt in another language and country."

Is translation at all possible? For some, art cannot be translated, while for others, for instance, Joyce or Pound, anything can be translated. Santoyo (1996,

40) remarks, however, on Pound's heirs exercising their right to choose specialists to revise his translations. Translation theory has since early on considered the middle ground between free and literal translations to be the optimum translation strategy (e.g. Dryden). For Larson translation is a transference of meaning with a change of form; the ultimate goal of the translator being to produce an idiomatic translation, one that "does not sound like a translation" (1998, 18-19). Larson's proposed continuum is represented in Figure 1.1.

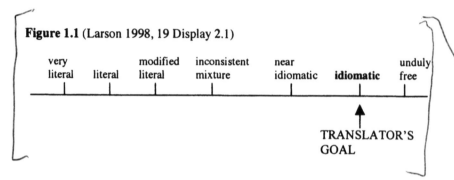

Figure 1.1 (Larson 1998, 19 Display 2.1)

| very literal | literal | modified literal | inconsistent mixture | near idiomatic | **idiomatic** | unduly free |

TRANSLATOR'S GOAL

Context is helpful in decision-making as does ascertaining the type of text one is translating; for example, it is not uncommon for children's stories to have formulaic expressions that have exact replicas in another language, such as *Once upon a time – Érase una vez.* There are many text typologies and while some can fit into more than one category, studies such as those by Reiss (1989, 2000) or Newmark (1982) agree on the differentiation between expressive texts[5] (poems, novels, plays), in which aesthetics is the most salient feature, and informative texts (newspapers, directions, technical and scientific literature), where accuracy of the information is more relevant (informative texts are supposedly easier to translate once the lexicon is mastered.) A third category comprises vocative or operative texts, which intend a reaction from the reader, and include religious or political-type texts; here it is the appeal that the translator must try to replicate. (Reiss gives the example of the version of the Eskimo *Lord's Prayer* which says "Give us this day our daily fish.") Multi-media texts, a fourth text type Reiss added later with Vermeer in 1984, are those supplemented by other media, such as songs or comics. Snell-Hornby (1995, 32) displays text types following an 'integrated' approach to the field of translation (see figure 1.2).

A central issue in the process of translation is the unit of translation ("the smallest segment of the utterance whose signs are linked in such a way that they should not be translated individually," Vinay and Darbelnet 1995, 21) because of its range of interpretation. The more experienced the translator, the bigger the unit of translation (even the entire text). Less experienced translators, on the other hand, choose smaller units of translation, especially at the semantic or linguistic level.

Figure 1.2 Text type and relevant criteria for translation (Snell-Hornby 1995, 32)

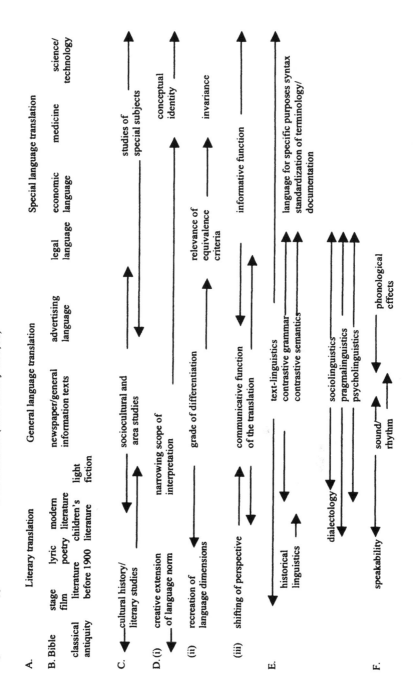

Text types

As Larson (1998, 17) explains "Because a given text has both form and meaning... there are two kinds of translations. One is form-based and the other is meaning-based." In fact, there are a great variety of TT forms which result from the purpose or function for which a translation is envisioned, the person commissioning the translation or the translator, and even from the use to which it is put. Following is an alphabetical list of the main translation types:

• Absolute translation

Absolute translations emphasize accuracy of content and form in the transference to a TL. Although a misnomer, an exaggeration or a futile and elusive ideal, it is a term used to distinguish between types of translations professionals write for clients, in apposition to abstract, diagrammatic, keyword (only key words are translated to see if the text merits a complete translation), reconstruction (a translation into a simple TL), selective (only selected passages are translated) and sight translations (Gouadec 1989).

• Abstract translation

Abstract translations are summarized versions of a source text in translation.

• Adaptation

Adaptations are considered to be free versions or imitations resulting from translational action. Already in the third century B.C. Livius Andronicus (c.285 - 204 B.C.) produced a target-oriented Latin adaptation of Homer's *Odyssey* (800 B.C.). In the 17th and 18th centuries, adaptations made to fit the literary and cultural tastes of the moment became popular again and in France these beautiful but 'unfaithful' texts became known as *belles infidèles*. Today many scientific and technical texts are adapted in translation for non-scientific readers.

• Auto-translation

The list of self- or auto-translators, i.e. writers who translate their own writing, is a long and impressive one: Rabindranath Tagore, Samuel Beckett, Jorge Luis Borges, Vladimir Nabakov, Umberto Eco, Guillermo Cabrera Infante, María Luisa Bombal or Rosario Ferré to name but a few. Self-translations, either simultaneously translated while the original is being written, or delayed until after the original has been published, vary in the degree of author intervention. Many self-translators such as María Luisa Bombal use the translation to include additions and corrections. James Joyce, who helped translate "Anna Livia Plurabella" (a section of the future *Finnegan's Wake*), made the Italian version more explicit; according to Jacqueline Risset (1984, 3) there is more slang, and different double and triple puns, all in all "a more daring variation." Rosario Ferré's novels in English, which she considers a "second chance" to fix mistakes, are translations of the ones she writes in Spanish. It is interesting to note that her *House on the Lagoon* does not acknowledge anywhere the original Spanish, *La casa de la laguna.* Stavans (1995, 640) considers this literary bilingualism "emblematic of her island's [Puerto Rico] disjointed soul."

Auto-translations can be regarded as more prestigious than 'regular' translations in part because they are not considered copies. In *The Subversive Scribe*, Levine, the renowned translator of Guillermo Cabrera Infante and Manuel Puig, explains that authors such as these who 'abuse' their own language and who consider their originals "translations of realities" tend towards more subversive translations. A case in point is Cabrera Infante, who confesses to not feeling any responsibility in English: Cabrera Infante has published three versions of *Vista del amanecer en el trópico:* the original Spanish (1974), a translation by Levine (1978), and a revised self-translation edition published a decade later spurred by his distaste of what he said sounded too much like Ernest Hemingway, and to which he added material.

• Crib translation
    A crib translation is a literal translation or the first draft of a translation. A crib translation used as a study aid is called a pony.

• Diagrammatic translation
    In a diagrammatic translation a text is transposed into a diagram.

• Ethnographic translation
    An ethnographic translation interprets and comments on the cultural context of the source text in the target text and is considered useful in the cross-cultural research so necessary to fields such as advertising.

• Exegetic translation
    An exegetic is one that explains, and therefore expands, the source text. Also called an annotated translation; it is the opposite of a gist translation.

• Fan translation
    A fan translation refers to the translation of video or computer games by players themselves into languages that the manufacturing companies do not translate into. Fan translations began with the translation of Japanese video games; the translation of the subtitles of games is called fansub.

• Full translation
    Full translation is understood to be the complete translation of a text, one in which no part of the ST language remains in the TT. Catford (1965, 21) explains that a full translation is one in which "every part of the SL text is replaced by the TL text material."

• Gist translation
    A gist translation is a rough outline of a translation; because it is a faster process, it is cheaper.

• Gloss translation
    A gloss translation, which oftentimes includes notes, is a translation that reproduces the form and content of the source text in the most literary and

meaningful way possible so the TT reader can "understand as much as he can of the customs, manner of thought, and means of expression" of the SL context (Nida, 1964:159). Because gloss translations offer deeper insights into the culture and language of the text, they are frequently used as study guides.

• Graphological translation[6]
A graphological translation substitutes the graphological units from one language into another. Because graphological translation does not necessarily produce a 'correct' translation, it is considered an extreme or exotic form of translation, used in poetry or advertising. For example: "the Russian word СПУТПИК can be graphologically translated into the Roman form CHYTHNK by substituting Cyrillic letters not with the nearest Roman sound equivalents, but with those Roman letters which most closely resemble them in appearance" (Shuttleworth and Cowie 1997, 68).

• Indirect translation
Indirect translations, also called second-hand or pivot translations, are translations of a source text, not directly from it, but via another translation. Through indirect translations, the language, culture, values, and ultimately canon of the intermediate culture enter the target culture, as was so common in colonial situations in which English or Spanish were the intermediate languages.

• Interlineal translation
An interlineal translation is an extreme case of literal translation as it attempts a word for word grammatical correspondence between the ST and the TT, used in language teaching or linguistics.

• Interlinear translation
Interlinear translation is a translation (or word for word glossary) of the ST located on the line under the original and is used as an aid in an extremely close reading of a ST or in language learning.

• Interlinguistic translation
An interlingual translation is translation proper, that is, between different languages, as apposed to intralingual or intersemiotic translation (see below).

• Intermediate translation
An intermediate translation is the translation that serves as a ST for an indirect translation.

• Intersemiotic translation
According to Jackobson (1992) besides interlinguistic and intralinguistic translation there exists intersemiotic translation, which involves the translation between a non-verbal and a verbal language (e.g.: OK and a thumbs up). This meaning has expanded to include, for example, adaptations of literary texts into film.

• Intertemporal translation

   Intertemporal translation is the interlinguistic or intralinguistic modernization of texts, as apposed to the less frequent archaization of texts.[7] An ongoing debate in translation studies is how older texts should be translated: should they be translated to a cotemporal linguistic equivalent of the original and risk incomprehension or should texts be linguistically updated and allow for comprehension? Another concern is what to do with cultural references and implications that have lost their meaning today- should these also be translated culturally, annotated, or left as is? Some scholars believe that the incorporation of some archaic features is one way to maintain a historical link or connection to the original.

• Intralingual translation

   An intralingual translation can be a rewording, a paraphrase or a translation into the same language of the source text but in a different variety or dialect. For instance, it is not uncommon for U.S. TV programs to be translated into the Spanish of Spain as well as into another variety of Spanish spoken in Latin America, also called localization.

• Parallel translation

   A parallel text is a translation alongside its source text; an extreme case being the Rosetta Stone, written in the three scripts spoken in Egypt when it was carved in 196 B.C.: Egyptian hieroglyphics, demotic (simplified hieroglyphics) and Greek.

• Parenthetic translation

   A parenthetic translation is a translation in parenthesis usually of just a word or phrase and is such a common practice in postcolonial literatures that Aschroft, Griffiths and Tiffin in *The Empire Writes Back* consider it the "most common authorial intrusion in cross-cultural texts" (1989, 61).

• Partial translation

   By partial translation Catford (1965, 21) denotes translations in which "some part or parts of the SL text are left untranslated" in the TT, often to produce an exotic feeling or more local flavor. Margaret Jull Costa's translation of Arturo Pérez Reverte's *El maestro de esgrima* (*The Fencing Master*) in English offers the following example: "On the corners, sellers cried their wares *Horchata de chufa*, delicious *horchata de chufa!*"

• Phonemic translation

   Phonemic or homophonic translations attempt to mimic the sound, rhythm and syntax of the source text language, blending both languages and allowing the "sense to emerge as a kind of vaguely suggested impression" (Hervey et al 1995, 48). The result can produce extremely foreignized texts.

• Phonological translation
   In a phonological translation, while grammar and lexis do not change, "the SL phonology of a text is replaced by the equivalent TL phonology" (Catford 1965, 56).

• Pseudotranslation
   A pseudotranslation is a fictitious translation that an author presents as a translation. One of the most famous is *El ingenioso hidalgo Don Quijote de la Mancha,* whose author Miguel de Cervantes presents as a Spanish translation he had commissioned from a collection of notebooks he found in a market in Toledo written in Arabic by El Cid Hamete Benengeli.

• Sight translation
   Sight translation is the oral translation of a written discourse.

• Transcription
   Transcription preserves the form of the ST in the TL and is usually used for names which have no equivalent in the TL. Transcription is also used to refer to interlingual translations into different mediums, for example from oral to written.

• Transliteration
   Transliteration is the transference of SL phonological units/writing systems into TL phonological units. This is more of an issue with certain languages than with others; for example, Russian, Chinese or Japanese into Romance languages.

----

1. Section II of The Translator's Charter of the International Federation of Translators (1994, 16) refers to the rights of translators, and states that:
15. The translator is therefore the holder of copyright in his/her translation and consequently has the same privileges as the author of the original work.
16. The translator shall thus enjoy, with respect to his/her translation, all the moral rights of succession conferred by his/her authorship.
2. The amalgamation of Greek plays into a Roman one is known as "contamination."
3. In the influential *After Babel,* Steiner (1975, 312-435) describes the hermeneutic motion in translation as one of 1) trust, 2) aggression or penetration, 3) incorporation, embodiment or appropriative use, and 4) compensation, restitution or fidelity. Steiner's sexually charged description of the translation process has been widely criticized.
4. While English does not distinguish between the directionality of translation, Spanish, Italian, Portuguese, Arabic and Chinese use the term direct translation to indicate translation into a person's mother tongue. Inverse translation, also called prose or service translation, is a translation from one's A language into one's B language.
5. According to Levine (1991, 7), translation exposes the subtexts of a text (the implied or unconscious version), which "may be as important as what it articulates."
6. Catford (1964, 22) considers graphological and phonological translation restricted translation because translation does not take place at all levels of the text.
7. Archaisms are used to give a translation a more poetic quality. In Bassnett's opinion (2002) the use of this 'pretend' language was a way to "colonize the past." Translators should beware of producing incongruent anachronistic translations, that is, using words

that are not in their time period, either with contemporary words in older texts or antiquated words in modern texts, unless it is as a foreignizing strategy.

Chapter 2

Translation Strategies and Techniques

Translations either relay the source text with the nuances of the original, or they are target-reader oriented and adapt to the language and culture of the TL. This binary difference has received a myriad of terms by translator scholars: Schleiermacher (1813) wrote of the distinction between naturalization and alienation, Vinay and Darbelnet (1958) of direct and indirect or oblique procedures, Nida (1964) of dynamic and formal equivalence, Catford (1965) wrote about the difference of cultural and linguistic translations, House (1977) of overt and covert translations, and Newmark (1991) called the result of the difference in translation techniques semantic and communicative translation. According to House, a covert translation attempts functional equivalence and aspires to sound like an original (if need be with a 'cultural filter') and "to recreate, reproduce or represent in the translated text the function the original has in its linguacultural framework and discourse world" (House 1997, 114). However, it is Houses's opinion that an overt translation does not attempt to sound like an original because, while many features can be equivalent (such as register or genre), the function of the new text cannot. Table 2.1 offers a summarized version of Newmark's (1991, 11-13) distinction between semantic and communicative features in translation, which encompasses in a broad manner the two main translation strategies used by translators.

Table 2.1 (Newmark 1991, 11-13)

Semantic translation	Communicative translation
Author-centered	Reader-centered
Semantic- and syntactic-oriented	Effect-oriented
Faithful, more literal	Faithful, freer
Meaning	Message

More awkward, more detailed	More natural, smoother but longer
Source-language based	Target-language based
Over-translated	Under-translated
Culture of original remains original	Culture of original is made more accessible
More powerful	Less powerful
The translator has no right to improve or correct	The translator has the right to improve, correct and clarify
Mistakes are in footnotes	Mistakes are corrected
Translation unit: tends to words, collocations and clauses	Translation unit: tends to sentences and paragraphs
The target: an exact statement	The target: a successful act
Translation is an art	Translation is a craft

An overview of the main translation strategies and techniques is extremely useful for the student of translation as these create awareness of the possibilities of procedures in the translation process and the consequences of one or another on the TT. The techniques are many and varied, and depend on a vast array of factors, which include the linguistic and cultural, the translator, the reader or the purpose of the translation. The techniques listed below are based significantly on Vinay and Darbelnet's work (1958, translated in 1995). This list of translation strategies is independent of the form-based translation types described in Chapter 1. They follow a continuum that ranges from the word level to the message itself, and from the specific to the general.

• Literal translation
     Literal translations are possible in simple sentences, the closer the languages involved (e.g.: *The movie is long* > *La película es larga* or *Háblame en inglés* > *Talk to me in English*). However, as soon as the words are embedded in polysemic structures this ceases to be the case (e.g.: *Háblame en cristiano* > *Talk to me in Christian,* i.e.: *Talk to me in a language I understand*). Machine translation is limited still at the beginning of the 21st century because it is not able to interpret all the possible combinations (e.g.: *Mr. Bush gave up running when he hurt his knee.* > *Sr. Bush dio para arriba el funcionamiento cuando él lastimó su rodilla* (http://www.systranbox.com/systran/box) and *Sr. Arbusto renunció corriendo cuando él dolió la rodilla* (http://ets.freetranslation.com/) or

Once upon a time > *Érase una vez* (http://www.systranbox.com/systran/box) but *Una vez que sobre un tiempo* (http://www.systranbox.com/systran/box)).

• Borrowings
When equivalence is not possible at the word level, Vinay and Darbelnet (1995) realize the need to borrow words from the source language and use them in the TL. While some are necessary because the concept may not exist in the TL (for example, because it is a new field, such as in the area of technology e.g.: *chip* in Spanish), others are not necessary. There has been a concerted effort to minimize the use of foreign words, especially from English, and allow them to take over existing forms (e.g. *espónsor* instead of *patrocinador*). However, newer Anglicisms from the world of technology (e.g. *internet*) are much more powerful than their literal Spanish translations (e.g. *red*). Oftentimes, translators are to blame for the entrance of borrowings or loanwords into a language.

Borrowings from English are called Anglicisms and those from Spanish Hispanicisms, and both are considered naturalized once they appear in dictionaries (new words that enter a language as a borrowing, a calque or an invented word are called neologisms). Anglicisms extend to phrases or syntactic structures as well; such as the use of the short, coordinated sentences of English in Spanish instead of the longer subordinated ones natural to the Spanish language. Recognizable Hispanicisms in English are *corral, burro, flan, machismo, mosquito, tortilla,* or the abbreviation *lb.* < *libra*. As García Yebra (1984, 335) states so aptly, while some are inevitable and others are not, there is no language that does not have some foreign words, adapted (linguistically or semantically).

• Calques
Calques translate a foreign or SL structure literally into the TL (e.g.: *kindergarten* > *jardín de infancia, skyscraper* > *rascacielos, sangre azul* > *blue-blood*).

• Transposition
Transposition is the transformation of a ST word into another grammatical category in the TT for equivalency in meaning (e.g.: from adjective to noun: *The Mexican border* > *La frontera con México*). In *Introducción a la traductología,* Vázquez Ayora (1977) supplies a long list of transposition types, organized by grammatical categories; e.g. verb > adverb (e.g. *It kept raining during our vacation* > *Llovía de continuo durante las vacaciones*), noun > verb (e.g. *Without the slightest hesitation* > *Sin vacilar en lo más mínimo*), adverb > verb (e.g. *He was never bothered again* > *Nadie volvió a molestarlo*), possessive pronoun > definite article (e.g. *Your hands are cold* > *Tienes las manos frías*), etc. López et al (2003) speak of crossed transposition when two terms take on each other's category, something that occurs frequently between adjectives and adverbs (e.g. *the idea was incoherently delightful* > *la idea era deliciosamente incoherente*).

• Modulation
According to Vinay and Darbelnet, modulation is a change in the point of view or image due to the difference between linguistic systems or cultures. Some examples include: Health *insurance* – *Seguro de* enfermedad; *Se lava* la cabeza *todos los días* – *S/He washes* her/his hair *everyday*; *life imprisonment* – *cadena perpetua*.

• Equivalence
Equivalence is a somewhat fuzzy category as essentially all translations look to be equivalent and transmit the same situation, if need be with other words, another structure or style. For Newmark (1991), who lists translation procedures according to their closeness to the source language, while there may be perfect equivalence (e.g.: *viernes* – *Friday*), it is "fruitless to define equivalence – a common academic dead-end pursuit" (3). Vinay and Darbelnet, on the other hand, call equivalence the strategy necessary in translating proverbs, expressions, plays on words or jokes (e.g.: *Men at work* > *Obras*; *Caution. Slippery when wet* > *Atención. Piso mojado; Llueve a cántaros* > *It's raining cats and dogs*.)

• Adaptation
Adaptation –which can include anything from the transcription of the original, to updating a translation, omission, expansion, exoticism or situational equivalence– is another controversial issue due to its domesticating (or naturalizing) nature. Many ST elements different from the target culture are easily erased following a translator's ideology or sense of decorum. For example, Lefevere (1992a, 41-2) has gathered the varied translations of *penis* in Aristophanes' *Lysistrata* "if he doesn't give you his hand, take him by the penis" (literally) as *membrum virale, leg, nose, handle, prick, life-lines, anything else*. Lefevere (1992a, 42) expresses his concern that "the translation projects a certain image of the play in the service of a certain ideology." López et al (2003) provide an example of a sonnet by Shakespeare in which *summer* has been translated as *primavera* to adapt the situation to a Spanish audience for whom the elements associated with an English summer are actually more associated with Spain's spring. According to Vinay and Darbelnet (1995), adaptation is necessary when cultural situations are so different that connotations are lost; for example, their famous example of a recreational event such as the *Tour de France* for which they suggest *cricket* as an English equivalent. Edward Fitzgerald's liberal English version from Farsi of the *Rubaiyat of Omar Khayyam* is considered one of the most beautiful translations of all times in part due to the fact that, like other Romantics, Fitzgerald believed effect was more important than accuracy or fidelity. (He is infamous, however, for his comments that Persian poetry was only beautiful when translated into English.)

• Paraphrase
According to Webster's New Collegiate Dictionary, paraphrase is "a restatement of a text, passage, or work giving the meaning in another form." For Dryden, paraphrase was the perfect middle ground in translation, a strategy

between imitation or word for word translation (which he called metaphrase). Three hundred years later, Newmark (1991) calls it "the loosest translation procedure, which simply irons out the difficulties in any passage by generalizing" (3), while Robinson (2004) extends the term to cover intralingual translations, i.e. versions of translations in the same language (167).

• Compensation
Compensation is a procedure by which a translator adds information (linguistic, cultural, stylistic) in one part of the TT, which was lost in another part of the ST to avoid translation loss.

• Expansion or amplification
Expansion or amplification is the use of a greater number of words in the TL than in the SL. While expansion can be the result of a non-correspondence between linguistic structures (e.g. *La niña* estrenó *los zapatos en la boda de su hermana* > *The girl* wore *her new shoes* for the first time *at her sister's wedding*), there are cases in which text expansion results from a translator's own personal sense of creativity. Such is the case of *The Thousand and One Nights,* which has had stories added in the process of translation: first, in the 9th century translation from Farsi into Arabic and then, in 14th century when another translator adds the famous Sherezade story.

Santoyo (1996, 49) remarks on a translation into Spanish of Walter Scott's *Quintin Durward,* which eliminates the author's prologue and the introductory chapter, and then riddles the new text with the translator's own literary additions and inventions. For example:

Before the period she had to struggle for her every existence with the English, already possessed of her fairest provinces.[1]

Mucho antes de esta época se veía ya precisada a sostener contra Inglaterra, dueña de sus mejores provincias, continua y sangrienta lucha, tratándose nada menos que de defender su existencia política.[2]

• Explicitation
Explicitation, generally believed to be unnecessary, is a strategy that tends towards specificity. As explicitation explains in translation that which is implicit in the SL, the result is a more redundant and cohesively explicit TT. An example at the level of the text is the inclusion of a family tree 'explaining' the family relationships of Gabriel García Márquez's *Cien años de soledad* (*A Hundred Years of Solitude*) in the English version but absent in the original Spanish.

• Undertranslation
Undertranslation, also called simplification, is a generalization of the ST in the TL because of loss of linguistic or cultural meaning.

• Omission
    It is not infrequent for target texts to have a number of omissions, and, as in the case of expansion, this can de due to a lack of one-to-one correspondence between languages or cultures or (why not?) to the whimsy of a translator. How else to understand Isabel Allende's English version of *La casa de los espíritus* in which "*atravesado por* media docena *de flechas*" becomes "*pierced by arrows*"? Venuti believes that more often than not translators will erase notions that he or she believes will not suit the new readers' sensibilities, such as references to sexual behaviors. In the Middle Ages, the *Escuela de Traductores* of Toledo used omissions to christianize Arab texts in the Latin translations. For Santoyo (1996, 39), an extreme case of omission is a Spanish translation published in Chile in 1972 of *Lady Chatterly's Lover* which is missing more than 25 percent of D. H. Lawrence's original.

---

1. Walter Scott *Quintin Durward*, Everyman: London, Dent and Sons, 1960, 35.
2. Walter Scott *Quintin Durward*, Madrid: Editorial Ramón Sopena, 1957, 7.

Chapter 3

History of Translation Theories

From the first work on translation in 46 B.C. by Cicero to the 1950s, writings about translation have dealt, on the one hand, with what constitutes a 'good' translation and, on the other hand, with the debate between literal versus free translation. In the 20th century, approaches to translation became more linguistically oriented and centered on the issue of equivalence. By the 1970s, translation theories were orienting themselves towards functional and communicative issues, and distinguishing between text types and their purpose, and by the 1980s discourse analysis, register and sociocultural factors began to dominate the theoretical realm. The 1990s and the beginning of the 21st century saw the steady rise of translation studies as an academic discipline as it paralleled the growth of cultural studies. A chronological study of the craft of translation becomes a window into the cultural history of the world and exposes the role of translation as a tool in bridging cultures and expanding literatures.

Pre-twentieth century

The first Western writers to leave an account of their approach to translation are Cicero and Horace. Both were part of the Roman tradition of using the exercise of translation as a means of expanding literary expertise and of translating into Latin the Greek works that were so locally favored. These two men were to wield enormous influence on translation strategies for hundreds of years for preferring what they called a sense for sense translation over a more literal or word for word translation. Marco Tulio Cicero (106-43 B.C.) was a Roman writer, politician, lawyer and translator whose *De optimo genere oratorum* (*The Best Kind of Orator*) in 46 BC displayed his approach to translation. In this introduction to one of his own translations, Cicero explains that he shies away from the prevailing Latin tradition of word for word translations alongside the original Greek, his preference being a "language which conforms to our usage," because he states "If I render word for word, the result will sound uncouth." Horace (Quintus Horatius Flaccus, 65-8 B.C.) agreed with Cicero and in "Ars Poetica" (20 B.C.?) also advised against a translation that rendered the "original word for word like a slavish translator." For Horace the aesthetic quality of a translation should be stressed over the fidelity to the original.

The Bible is both the largest translation project in history and a source of great religious, political and linguistic controversy. It is divided into two main sections: the Old Testament (also called the Hebrew Bible), which pre-dates the birth of Christ, written mainly in Hebrew with some Aramaic, and the New Testament, written in Greek (probably between 50 and 125 A.D.). The translation of the Bible has remained controversial: while some believe that it is God's word and should be translated word for word, others believe everyone should have access to a sense for sense translation in an intelligible language. Further controversies stem from debates about the appropriate source version on which to base biblical translations.

The most famous Bible story that pertains to languages is the Tower of Babel (Genesis 11: 1-9) the myth of one language and, by extension, the origin of translation. The Old Testament story starts with a monolingual world in which humans decide to build a city called Babel and then a tower to reach the heavens. God considers this a temerity and punishes humans with many languages, so they cannot understand each other, and they are unable to finish the tower.[1]

The first translation of the Bible took place in the third century B.C. This translation of the Old Testament from the original Hebrew and Aramaic into Koine, a popular Greek dialect spoken in the Eastern Mediterranean during Roman times, is called the *Greek Septuagint Version* because of the 70 translators who supposedly worked its translation. As the Christian faith spread in the Roman Empire, a version in Latin was needed and by the end of the 2nd century A.D., there were versions in Italy and in northern Africa. It is at the behest of Pope Damascus I, who wanted a uniform Latin text that Jerome acquiesced to its translation. His version, written between 382 and 404 from the Hebrew and Greek originals, is called the *Vulgate Bible*. Jerome not only undertook a sense for sense translation but decided against a formal Latin in favor of a vulgar Latin. The fact that Jerome's *Vulgate* became the source text for most translations of the Bible until recently (and remains the official Latin Bible of the Roman Catholic Church) is a testament to its significance for over 1500 years.[2]

As vernacular literatures developed, so did translations of the Bible. Bassnett explains that writers used translation as "a means of increasing the status of their own vernacular" (Bassnett 2002, 57), and the idea that the common people should have access to the Scriptures became a central demand of the Reformation. Sections of the Bible were translated into Goth, Slavonic, French, and Catalan. After Erasmus's new translation into Latin in 1516, Martin Luther (1486-1546) undertook his own translation of the Bible into vulgate German, the East Middle German which ultimately became the national standard. Nowhere is the centrality of Bible translation in the world's events more clearly exemplified than in the consequences of Luther's translation of 1534, which ultimately led to a break with the Roman Catholic Church and to the establishment of the Protestant Church.

The first translation of the Bible into English was written by John Wycliffe between 1380 and 1384. However, the most influential version in English is the *King James Bible* of 1611 (also known as the *Authorized Version*), largely based on another English version published in 1525/6, undertaken by William Tyndale directly from the Greek and Hebrew. The importance of Tyndale's version lies not only in the fact that most subsequent English translations are based on it but that so many English writers have quoted from his version, thereby influencing English literature substantially.

The consequences of a 'heretic' translation could be extreme: Tyndale, who strove to make the Bible more accessible, would ultimately pay for his 'heretic' translation by being burned at the stake in 1536. Similarly, Étienne Dolet (1509-1546), an academic and printer, was accused of heresy for his own translation of the Bible into French. When the Sorbonne University accused Dolet of producing a translation of Plato's that seemed to question man's immortality, he was later burned at the stake. Translation was so central for Dolet that in *La maniere de bien traudire d'une langue en aultre* (1540) he lays out 5 guiding principles for translators. According to the Frenchman, translators should: 1) understand the text perfectly, 2) know the target language and source language perfectly, 3) avoid word for word translations, 4) avoid Latin or other strange forms, and 5) attempt to be eloquent.

The first complete translation of the Bible into Spanish was published in 1569 and was undertaken by Casiodoro de Reina. This version, which became the basis for most subsequent translations into Spanish, is known as *The Bear Bible* (*Biblia del Oso*) because of the bear on its cover. All Spanish versions, including Cipriano de Valera's revision in 1702, were banned in Spain and read only by Protestants until the Inquisition finally allowed the publication of the Bible in Spanish in 1782. In 1790 Felipe de Scío y Riaza published a Spanish-Latin version (*Biblia de Scío*) which appeared in Mexico in 1831. The Bible has been translated into many lesser known languages and at least some part of the Bible has been translated into the 2009 languages and dialects which are spoken by 97% of the world's population. Today, one of the major organizations dedicated to the translation of the Bible is the Wycliffe Bible Translators, an organization that has already overseen complete translations of the Bible into 400 languages.

In a context such as this, it is imperative to mention *La Escuela de Traductores de Toledo* (The Toledo School of Translators), which evolved in the 12th century from the desire to make the scientific and philosophical knowledge of the Greeks (for example, Aristotle) available to the rest of Europe. The Arabs had translated, studied and annotated these works for centuries. *La Escuela de Traductores de Toledo* is best known for the collaborative work of Christians, Muslims and Jews who translated together in libraries and the cathedral, oftentimes sight translating orally from the Arab or Hebrew into Medieval Spanish and then writing the Latin translation. By the 13th century and under King Alfonso X the Wise, the translations were rendered solely into Spanish, significantly strengthening the language.[3] In the 7th century, on the other side of the world, Xuan Zang spent 17 years in India looking for Buddhist scriptures. The rest of his life he spent translating from Sanskrit scriptures and the 657 scrolls he had brought back from India (84 times longer than the Bible) with his assistants in the translation school he set up in Chang'an.[4]

By the 1600s, translators were increasingly taking liberties with classical texts; for example, Abraham Cowley (1618-67) states that he has "taken, left out, and added what I please."[5] The growing influence of these 'imitators' led John Dryden (1631-1700) to put forth in the preface to his own translation of *Ovid's Epistles* (1680) a typology of translation according to the degree of closeness to the source text. Dryden explained that imitations in the style of contemporaries of the translator and metaphrase or "word by word and line by line" translations, which he said was like "much like dancing on ropes with fettered legs – a foolish task," were "the two extremes which ought to be avoided." Dryden advocated paraphrase, which he explained as a sense for sense "translation with latitude, where the author is kept in view by the translator, so as never to be lost, but his words are not so strictly followed as his sense."

By the 18th century, translation strategies were shifting from the process of translation to the source text, metaphorically referred to as a portrait, with the translator being the painter. Alexander Tytler (1747-1813) wrote the first major work on translation in English. In "Essay on the Principles of Translation" (1797), Tytler set forth his own principles of translation, namely that 1) the translation should have all the information of the original, 2) the style of the translation should be like that of the source text, and 3) the translation should flow and be as easy to read as the original.

In "Über die verschiedenen Methoden des Überstzens" (1813) ("On the different methods of translating"), the Austrian Romantic Friedrich Schleiermacher (1768-1834) wrote of the translation strategies needed for different types of texts. It was his belief that translations should take the reader to the author (later called foreignization), not the author to the reader (later called domestication) that was to become a major influence on subsequent translation theories.

Twentieth century

Gradually, translation theories in the 20th century became much more linguistically oriented and centered on equivalence, an important issue in translation (see Chapter 1). However, it was not until the second half of the century that translation theory gained the momentum that it enjoys today. The issue of equivalence is taken up by the structuralist Roman Jackobson, for whom equivalence is not to be found at a lexical or syntactic level ("translation involves two equivalent messages in two different codes" 1992, 146), but at a conceptual one: "Languages differ essentially in what they must convey and not in what they can convey" (1992, 149). Jackobson recognizes, though, that "only rarely can one reproduce both content and form in a translation, and hence in general the form is usually sacrificed for the sake of the content." The well-known linguist and influential scholar and translator of the Bible, Eugene Nida (1964, 159) makes a distinction between equivalence of the form of a text (formal equivalence or correspondence) and the content, including cultural elements, and 'effect' (dynamic or functional equivalence). In *The Theory and Practice of Translation* (1969, 33), Nida and Charles Taber characterize translation and the process of equivalence as one in which a translator must analyze, transfer and restructure.

Figure 3.1 (Nida and Taber 1969, 3 Figure 6)

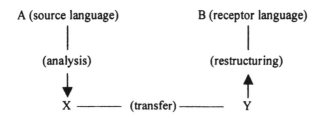

A (source language)   B (receptor language)

(analysis)   (restructuring)

X ———— (transfer) ———— Y

John C. Catford advocated a more linguistic approach to equivalence in translation, by introducing the concept of shifts of translation motivated by linguistic differences in the SL and TL. These shifts of translation are "departures from formal correspondence in the process of going from the SL to the TL" (1965, 73) or as Popovic (1970, 79) explains: "All that appears as new with respect to the original, or fails to appear where it might have been expected, may be interpreted as a shift." Catford identified obligatory shifts (imposed by the TL) and optional shifts (stylistic or cultural shifts that the translator chooses to incorporate or not).

In spite of the growth of translation studies, the notion of equivalence remains central to the field. Werner Koller draws on Saussure for his theory of equivalence of translation, explaining that untranslatability does not exist. For Koller equivalence occurs at the level of *parole*, between specific SL and TL items, and correspondence at the level of *langue*, between language systems.[6] Peter Newmark advocates text analysis according to intention, text types, intended reader, style, quality, cultural aspects, etc. as a way to determine a translation strategy. Newmark distinguishes between what he calls a semantic translation which "attempts to render. . . the exact contextual meaning of the original" (1988, 39) and communicative translation (see Chapter 2). He goes on to explain that "In general, a semantic translation is written at the author's linguistic level, a communicative at the readership's" (47). Similarly, Juliane House (1977) suggests evaluating a ST to determine its function so as to be able to replicate it in the TL. This functional equivalent is what she calls a covert translation. House explains that a covert translation could be the translation of an academic paper with no visible SL features, as opposed to the overtly obvious translation of a political speech in which cultural references might be unknown to the ST reader.

The importance of text types in translation is taken up by Katherina Reiss (1989), who distinguishes four text types: informative (technical, scientific), expressive (literary), operative (publicity), and multi-media or subsidiary (songs, dubbing, etc) (see Chapter 1). Following the notion of text types, Hans J. Vermeer formulated the theory of the skopos (Greek, for "aim" or "purpose") in

1978 and later expanded it with Reiss in 1984. According to the skopos theory, translation strategies depend not only on the purpose or function of a text in translation but also on the initiator of the translation project. However, there are those like Hatim and Mason who oppose the skopos theory of translation because it denies "the reader access to the world of the SL text" (1990, 9).

Comparative linguistic studies have focused on equivalence in specific languages. A case in point is Valentín García Yebra's *Teoría y práctica de la traducción* (1984), in which he compares Spanish to English, French and German structures in translation, and Gerardo Vázquez Ayora's *La traductología: Curso básico de traducción* (1977). A precursor to these was J. P. Vinay and J. Darbelnet's influential study on linguistic comparison and equivalence, *Stylistique comparée du français et de l'anglais* published in 1958 but not translated into English until 1995. Vinay and Darbelnet present seven specific translation strategies: the direct (or literal) translation strategies being 1) borrowing, 2) calque, 3) literal translation, and the oblique translation strategies being: 4) transposition, 5) modulation, 6) equivalence, and 7) adaptation (see Chapter 2). For Vinay and Darbelnet, equivalence is a necessary procedure in order to "replicate the same situation as in the original, whilst using completely different wording' (1995, 342).

The birth of a contemporary discipline
In 1972 James Holmes presented a now seminal paper called "The Name and Nature of Translation Studies" (not published until 1988) in which he argued for the term Translation Studies "as the standard term for the discipline as a whole" (Holmes 2000, 175). Although at first the term was used to refer more to literary translation, translation studies now extends to all the fields involved in translation.[7] Holmes outlined translation as a field made up of diverse academic disciplines, divided into theoretical, descriptive and applied branches. (See Figure 3.2.)

Figure 3.2 (Holmes's map, Toury 1995, 10)

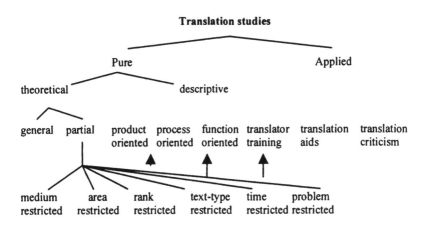

As the target text became a greater object of concern, Holmes, Theo Hermans, Gideon Toury and other members of the Manipulation School focused their attention on a descriptive approach to translation (Descriptive Translation Studies -DTS) to identify the literary, linguistic and social norms underlying the process of translation. They believed that "all translation implies a degree of manipulation of the source text for a certain purpose" (Hermans 1995, 217). George Steiner, Itamar Even-Zohar and Anthony Pym have written along these descriptive lines.

Translation studies in the last twenty or thirty years have become more socioculturally oriented; in the 1990s this development paralleled cultural studies quite closely. Susan Bassnett (1980/2002), André Lefevere (1992a, 1992b), Sherry Simon (1996), Gayatari Chakravorty Spivak (2003) and Lawrence Venuti (1995, 1998, 2000) are some of the most notable academics incorporating cultural studies issues such as gender, canons, post-colonialism, or ideology in translation studies.

Technological advances have radically changed translation, by offering easily accessible aids to translators although for Munday (2001, 191), these make the translator even more invisible, because any form of machine translation "conceals the human involvement and gives the impression of it being an easy and automatic process." Machine or computer translation is a controversial issue, in part because it has not become the success expected.

Machine translation can translate technical or scientific material relatively well, as the Canadian Meteorological Centre of Environment's MÉTÉO machine-translation system proves daily by translating 80,000 words of meteorological forecasts from French to English. But the main problem that computer translation comes up against is meaning, because words mean differently in different combinations, and, as of yet, computers cannot 'understand' all the different combinations that are possible. Aware that machine translation cannot offer 'perfect' equivalencies, massaging by human hands of machine-generated translations becomes a reality (so-called machine-aided translation or computer-aided translation, CAT). Machine aids for translators include on-line dictionaries, data bases and translation memory (TM) programs which assist the translator by suggesting possible translations and by 'remembering' how one has translated a sentence or phrase and 'reminding' the translator how s/he translated it before.

Where translation studies is headed is hard to tell; the 1990s saw a boom in the degrees offered in universities around the world, and while there are a few who fear it could disperse according to specific paradigms, most (e.g. Baker, 2004) seem to believe that if its growth as an academic field is any indication, it can only move forward.

---

1. The story of the Tower of Babel, one of whose etymologies in Hebrew is to *confuse*, can be read not only as the beginning of translation but also as a stand against linguistic diversity.
2. September 30th is the feast of St. Jerome and International Translation Day.
3. In 1994 the School of Translators reopened at the University of Castilla-La Mancha as a research center for Arab and Hebrew studies.
4. Xuan Zang is a renowned figure in China through the great classic Chinese novel called *Journey to the West,* loosely based on his life.
5. In the Preface to his *Pindarique Odes* (1656) as cited in Steiner (1975, 254).
6. For Koller (1979b) the analysis of linguistic function, content, style, formal, aesthetic and pragmatic characteristics of texts were important in determining translation strategies.
7. Other terms that have been used to refer to translation studies are: translatology, traductology or Science of Translation.

Chapter 4

Traduttore, traditore.
Shaping culture through translation

The Italian saying *traduttore, traditore* ("translator, traitor") is widely used to address the difficulty of the 'perfect' translation. Simultaneously, it brings forth the notion of untranslatability, a radical change of the meaning of the source text and language due to translation process (Pym and Turk 2001, 273). The theories of translatability and untranslatability revolve around the concept of meaning and its relation to thought processes. They operate around three notions: 1) meaning is universal, and therefore not tied to thought processes, allowing therefore for the translation of all texts, 2) thought processes and words are so interrelated that translation becomes an "impossible task" (Humboldt 1796), and 3) language is important in thought processes but regardless, texts should be translated (Pym and Turk 2001, 273-4). Therefore, what is lost in translation is not relegated to one lone aspect of language but to the philosophical, linguistic and methodological constructs that underlay human communication. Clearly, the closer the languages and the 'simpler' the message, the closer the translation; plays on words, puns, irony or allusions are less simple and so become highly untranslatable.

Regardless of the languages or texts involved, studies indicate (e.g. Baker 1993) that all translations share certain linguistic features such as simplification or explicitation, called universals of translation. No one denies that losses in translation, either linguistic or cultural, are inevitable; however, minimizing these and avoiding interference of the SL in the TL are the ideals of most translators. While interference is more noticeable at the word level through borrowings, calques, and neologisms, it also occurs at the syntactic level (and, of course, at the cultural level). Duff (1981) writes precisely of the constraints on target languages made by source language structures, for they can produce what he calls a 'third language', strange and unidiomatic; this odd language, where everything starts to sound the same, is also referred to as translationese. Translationese in turn is different from a controlled language, which is a "simplified version of a language" (Arnold et al 1994, 211) in its vocabulary and grammar and is used as a basis for machine translation.[1]

The process of transferring one language to another in translation has yet to be understood, but the fact is that both languages –the SL and the TL– are being processed in a translator's brain, similar to language processing in a bilingual's brain. In fact, Harris (1988) coined the term bi-text to refer to the psychological construct of a translator's mind being "simultaneously present and intimately interconnected" to the original and its translation in the translatorial process. This multi-presence of languages occurs as well in many post-colonial and immigrant literatures and is especially difficult to translate in the presence the 'other' language, as the sense of alterity or otherness almost all but disappears. In hybrid multilingual texts, otherness draws on the codeswitches, which are found glossed, italicized, explained or not translated at all, depending on the domesticating or foreignizing approach of the writer. These multilingual linguistic strategies are extremely challenging for translators, who must devise the most appropriate technique to transfer otherness to the other.

No one denies how literature has shaped culture; however, little attention until recently has been paid to the role of translation in this process or how it has shaped the make-up of canons across the world. Borges, for example, was well aware of how he was shaping the Latin American literary canon by the texts he chose to translate into Spanish, knowing they became references for writers and readers alike. Similarly, Venuti (1998) recounts how the Japanese literary canon in the United States from the 1950s to the 1990s was based almost exclusively on the Japanese writers that a handful of U.S. university professors had discovered and translated into English at the end of World War II.

As post-colonialism reviews the power relations between empires and their former colonies, translation is exposed as a major tool in this domination (as are publishing practices). According to Cheyfitz (1991, 112) "from its beginnings the imperialist mission is . . . one of translation: the translation of the 'other' into the terms of the empire." Translation is considered a metaphor of power because, as the discourse of the empire is strengthened, that of the post-colonial becomes a copy, and like all copies, second-class. A study on the prefaces and notes of English translations in the colonial period in India led Niranjana (1992, 2) to reveal the extent to which the colonized has been excluded from his/her own history: "What is at stake here is the representation of the colonized, who need to be produced in such a manner as to justify cultural domination." Niranjana (1992, 3) goes on to say:

> Translation thus produces strategies of containment. By employing certain modes of representing the other—which it thereby also brings into being—translation reinforces hegemonic versions of the colonized, helping them acquire the status of what Edward Said calls representations, or objects without history. These become facts exerting a force on events in the colony: witness Thomas Babington Macaulay's 1835 dismissal of indigenous Indian learning as outdated and irrelevant, which prepared the way for the introduction of English education.

The Americas, Africa, Asia and the Caribbean were colonized through language; by 1918, 85 percent of the world had been colonized by Europeans. Queen Isabel, who had been well aware of the importance of language in the reconquest of Spain from the Arabs, made sure that the first grammar of Spanish and the first written of a vernacular language was sent on Christopher Columbus'[2] first voyage. Anticipating his interlocutors, Columbus took a handful of interpreters with him; undeterred, on his trip back to Spain he brought with him almost a dozen men to train as interpreters for his subsequent trips. In Latin America the *mestizos* who could write were to become the translators and interpreters (called *lenguas*) between the colonizers and the colonized.

La Malinche (Malinalli Tenépal or Malintzin) is by far the most (in)famous translator in Latin America, vilified as interpreter and supposed bridge to the disappearance of the Aztec empire. Her story and the transformation she is undergoing today parallels that of translation, from underdog to darling. According to Bernal Diaz's 1568 firsthand account in *Historia verdadera de la conquista de la Nueva España (The True History of the Conquest of New Spain)*, Malintzin, rejected by her mother in favor of her younger half-brother, wound up in Tabasco and then was given to Hernán Cortés as a slave in 1519. Having learned Mayan in Tabasco, Malinalli was asked to interpret between the Spanish conquistador and Moctezuma when the Aztec emperor and the Spanish conquistador met: Moctezuma spoke Aztec to La Malinche, who interpreted into Mayan for the Spanish priest Don Jerónimo de Aguilar, who in turn relayed the message into Spanish, and then back again. (This is known today as consecutive relay interpretation). In time, Malinalli, or doña Marina as she later became known, learned Spanish and became the sole interpreter between Moctezuma and Cortés, with whom she would have a son, don Martín Cortés, considered the first Mexican mestizo. While Malinche (a nickname she received as she worked for Cortés) is regarded by many Mexicans a traitor (*malinchismo* has entered the Spanish dictionary as synonymous with a sale to foreigners), there are many voices clamoring to have La Malinche reinterpreted as a national figure, worthy of respect because of her linguistic abilities and intelligence, not the culprit responsible for the Spanish conquest of Mexico and downfall of the Aztec empire.

Due to what is referred to as the politics of translation, the languages of empires (e.g. Spanish and English) yield a strong hold over the philosophical and cultural discourse of their colonies as they become the 'original' to copy from. In this new space, in which translation constructs a new cultural representation, it happens that the foreignness in texts becomes domesticated. Without a doubt, this "illusion of originality" which Venuti refers to, is a consequence of the way in which the translation works to assimilate the source culture into the target culture.[3] Domesticated or naturalized translations are so fluent that they seem to be originals not only at the level of the word but also in the content– in direct opposition to exoticism or foreignization.[4] In 1813 Schleiermacher explained naturalization as a process in which:

Either the translator leaves the writer alone as much as possible and moves the reader towards the writer, or he leaves the reader alone as much as possible and moves the writer towards the reader.

Translation history is chock full of examples of SL texts being domesticated to fit the target culture: a sonnet by Shakespeare translated into Hebrew where the love between two men is transformed to that between a man and a woman in order to avoid references to homosexuality; the Roman translations of Greek literature in which the author's name is substituted by the translator's and the culture is adapted to that of the translator;[5] or intralingual translations, such as the U.S. versions of J.K. Rowling's Harry Potter series which adapt weights or measurements to the U.S. reader; or William Weaver's translation into English of Umberto Eco's *The Name of the Rose,* which omits 12 pages of Latin and medieval terms, presumably to fit English speakers' less cultured tastes.

Foreignization, also referred to as minoritizing, alienating, exoticising or documentary, is one viable strategy "toward a new practice of translation" (Niranjana 1992, 46). Foreignization involves the production of minoritizing translations that "promote cultural innovation as well as the understanding of cultural difference by proliferating the variables within English" (Venuti 1998, 11). As a translation strategy, minoritizing does not erase those elements that make a text foreign in the target language like domestication does; this translatorial strategy allows for the linguistic and stylistic features of a text to be 'read' in translation, although too close of a translation could result in non-comprehension. Today there is a certain tendency towards foreignizing not only in the translation of texts themselves but also in non-mainstream texts chosen for translation. Other foreignizing techniques are the juxtaposition of archaic and modern terms alongside each other, to call "attention to the translation as a translation without unpleasurably disrupting the reading experience" (Venuti 1998, 15) or transliteration (e.g.: Levine, who translates *Yo soy un hombre sincero* as *I'm a man without a zero*). Lewis (1985) takes foreignization a step further by advocating abusive fidelity in translation, a technique which involves experimentation and the manipulation of language. According to Berman (2003), because domestication does not preserve the foreign of a ST, translators should counterbalance these "deforming tendencies" through more literal translation. The twelve deforming strategies which alter the original according to Berman are:

• rationalization: texts are altered to fit features other than those of the ST (e.g.: grammatical categories are changed, such as the use of nouns for verbs)
• clarification: oftentimes meanings are clarified in translation even when the intention of the ST is to conceal them
• expansion: all translations are longer than their originals, overtranslated or "inflationist" (Steiner 1975)
• ennoblement (and popularization): translations are altered by 'elegant' rewriting (or slang)

• qualitative impoverishment: a TT is impoverished when terms, idioms, or expressions of less quality or "'iconic' richness" are used
• quantitative impoverishment: lexical loss or loss of ambiguity results from a translation having less signifiers than the original (e.g.: the use of only one word in the TT such as *face* for the varied *semblante, rostro,* and *cara* in the ST)
• destruction of rhymes: rhythms (in poetry, plays or novels) can be destroyed through punctuation (e.g. a short passage by Faulkner has 4 punctuation marks in the original, the translation 22, as noted by Gresset and Samway 1983)
• the destruction of underlying networks of signification: subtexts can disappear in translation
• the destruction of linguistic patterns: new linguistic patterns in translation can make translations seem more homogenous and/or inconsistent than the original
• the destruction of vernacular networks or their exoticization: Berman believes vernaculars cling "tightly to their soil" and that translation should only occur between "cultivated" languages; however, it is not uncommon for a southern drawl to be substituted for an Andalusian accent
• the destruction of expressions and idioms: equivalents are not translations but ethnocentric attempts
• the effacement of the superimposition of languages: for Berman the tension created between dialects, sociolects or idiolects and literary language demands major attention from translators, considering it as he does "the central problem posed by translating novels" (Berman 2003, 296).

Gayatri Spivak is an example of a translator who translates so that the differences of the subaltern, third world minority literature do not disappear in translation. Spivak's ethical commitment to the translation project is such that in her translations from Bengali into English of Mahasweta Devi, the Indian activist, she includes a translator's preface, an afterword, and end-notes. Generally, notes such as footnotes, endnotes, prefaces or introductions are supplementary features used by translators or editors to explain source features that might be unknown to target readers, such as historical and cultural facts or even linguistic expressions. Except in the more academic texts, where notes and footnotes can be copious, translators tend to use them as sporadically as possible because they are said to restrict readership. However, Sandra Cisnero's Spanish translation of *Caramelo* (2003) is worth mentioning here because the English version by Liliana Valenzuela includes notes by the translator and the editor on the translation project and the language, a significant editorial commitment with the readership.[6]

While translators such as Spivak use prefaces or forwards to resist cultural domination, and others such as Wycliffe, Cicero, Dryden or Valenzuela use them to explain translation strategies, there are others who utilize them to justify changes from the source text. In the preface to his translation of *The Thousand and One Nights,* Edward Lane explains that what is "wholly inappropriate for translation" or is "too coarse for translation," he has eliminated. Nida (1998) advocates the use of notes to explain cultural differences because any other solution would require a change of the source text.

In the translation process, more often than not, the 'other' is rewritten in the image of the Empire, and as a consequence of the 'power imbalance,' comparisons create the image of a colonial inferior, even at a national level. A case in point is the internal colonialism in Spain or the United Kingdom, which gave way to linguistic denigration: Catalan, Galician and Basque were considered inferior to Castilian Spanish (especially during Franco's regime) and Irish to English (Cronin 1996)[7] and not avoided as target languages.

Censorship in translation is imposed by political regimes as well as by single translators, who change target texts to adhere to supposed expectations of intended readers. For example, Santoyo (1996, 41) quotes Agustín Aicart's preface to Walter Scott's 1829 translation of the poem "The Vision of Don Roderick" ("La visión de don Rodrigo") in which the translator offers his reasons behind thought and character substitutions:

> Walter Sccoth [sic] es escocés y escribe principalmente para los ingleses: Yo soy católico y español y escribo principalmente para los españoles. No aspiro tampoco a la gloria de traductor.[8]

Likewise, George Chapman's (1608) or Alexander Pope's (1715) translation of the *Iliad* from which both men eliminated allusions to homosexuality in spite of the fact it was a common practice in Homer's time (Williams 1992, 102-4). Franco's regime in Spain (1939-1975) censored among many other things the translation of movies. One famous case is John Ford's *Mogambo* (1953) in which an adulterous relationship between Clark Gable, Ava Gardner and Grace Kelly becomes in its dubbed Spanish version an incestuous one. To remove the stigma of the illicit sexual relationship between Gardner and Gable, who are ex-lovers, the Spanish censors made Ava Gardner and Clark Gable brother and sister without realizing that at one point in the movie both Gable and Ava would come together in an extremely passionate kiss.

There is no doubt that "translation is fraught with compromise" (Hervey et al 1995, 27) and that to translate can feel like treason *–traduttore, traditore–* to the source language and text, but Valentín García Yebra sagely explains that:

> La regla de oro para toda traducción es, a mi juicio, *decir todo* lo que dice el original, *no decir nada* que el original no diga, y *decirlo todo con la corrección y naturalidad* que permita la lengua a la que se traduce. Las dos primeras normas compendian y exigen la fidelidad absoluta al contenido; la tercera autoriza la libertad necesaria en cuanto al estilo. La dificultad reside en aplicar las tres al mismo tiempo. Quien sepa hacerlo merecerá con toda justicia el título de traductor excelente.[9]

---

1. *Wikipedia*, the online encyclopedia (www.wikipedia.org) has articles translated into 229 languages, one of which is Simple English, written with only the most basic English

words. Directed at students, children and adults with learning disabilities, "Simple English is similar to English, but it uses only easy words."
2. Antonio Nebrija's *Gramática castellana* was published in 1492.
3. Domestication also includes strategies that modernize and update cultural references such as those that produced the irony that pervaded so many classical Greek works and which would require copious notes for the non-expert to understand today.
4. Newmark (1991, 4) calls sourcerers those who believe translations should be faithful to the source text, and targeteers those who believe the target text is more important than faithfulness to the source text.
5. Called a cultural translation, it transposes the cultural elements of a text to another culture.
6. Margaret Jull Costa's English translation, *The Fencing Master*, of Arturo Pérez Reverte's *El maestro de esgrima*, actually includes a translator's afterword acknowledging specific people for the help and "invaluable advice on fencing terminology" which she received.
7. A translation from a SL that has the same prestige as the TL is known as a horizontal translation and a vertical translation is one in which the SL has greater prestige than the TL.
8. *Walter Scoth [sic] is Scottish and writes primarily for the English: I am Catholic and Spanish, and I write primarily for Spaniards. It's not as if I were aspiring to be a translator.*
9. *The rule of thumb for any translation is, in my opinion, to say everything the original says, not to say anything the original does not say, and to say everything with the accuracy and naturalness that the source language allows. The first two norms involve and demand complete faithfulness to the content; the third allows for the necessary liberty in style. The difficulty resides in applying the three at the same time. Whoever can do this justifiably merits the title of excellent translator.*

Chapter 5

Interpretation and Audiovisual Translation

Interpretation

Oral translation, or interpretation as it is better known, has become a well-established and well-paid profession, increasingly in demand in our globalized world, even though it has always existed, especially in the political arena. A famous Egyptian image dating from 1350 B.C. of an interpreter standing between Horemheb, the Pharaoh who succeeded Tutankhamun, and the Syrian ambassador is supposedly the first 'tangible' evidence of the task of an interpreter.[1] However, it was only when consecutive interpretation was first used in 1919 in the post-war negotiations after World War I that interpretation, as it is known today, laid its foundations as a profession. In 1927 when Edward Filene, Gordon Finlay and Thomas Watson from IBM added microphones to conference interpretation, simultaneous interpretation was born. Interpretation as a profession received full recognition during the Nuremberg trials (1945-6) following World War II, as Léon Dorstet led a team of 12 interpreters interpreting from and into German, English, French and Russian; from there Dorstet went on to establish interpretation at the United Nations. In 1941 the first training center for interpretation was established: the School of Translation and Interpretation (*École de traduction et interprétation*, ETI) in Geneva, Switzerland.

In simultaneous interpretation, an interpreter delivers the SL text almost instantaneously (about two seconds after the speaker has begun) into the TL with no time for note-taking, from a booth preferably equipped with electronic equipment (headphones and a microphone). Simultaneous interpretation is the form most used in conference and legal settings as well as in diplomatic proceedings today, superceding consecutive interpretation. In these venues, simultaneous interpreters customarily interpret one way, into their A language; retour is the term for interpretation into a person's B language. When there are not enough interpreters for all the languages involved in a conference, relay interpretation is often the solution. Relay interpretation takes place in simultaneous interpretation situations and involves one interpreter (called the pivot) who listens to the speaker speaking in the L1 and interprets into an L2 not only for part of the public but also for the other interpreters who do not understand the L1 and who then interpret the L2 into an L3 or L4. This is a highly stressful job for the pivot because so much relies on her/him. Cheval interpretation is when two booths doing simultaneous interpretation switch back and forth at conference settings.

Consecutive interpretation involves an interpreter repeating a message to a target audience following the original speaker's utterance, but because consecutive interpretation requires a great deal of memory, interpreters must use note-taking to remember ideas, numbers or names. (While there are general rules to these, every interpreter develops his or her own annotation system.) In short consecutive interpretation, the interpreter may call a stop when required, while long consecutive interpretation may involve an utterance of up to 15 minutes. Whereas simultaneous interpretation is used increasingly worldwide, consecutive is used in bilateral commercial situations, high-level talks and negotiations, and presentations when professional interpretation settings are not available or too expensive. While in consecutive interpretation the interpreters must render the same content as precisely as possible, in summary interpretation the interpreter renders a summarized version of the original utterance.

There are at least eight other modes of interpretation.

• Community interpretation entails interpreting between service providers, such as hospitals, police or immigration officials, and their clients over the phone or face to face. It is now considered a profession, but frequently untrained family members, friends and volunteers continue to interpret in these venues. Community interpreters must interpret both ways and supply a cultural interpretation as well (i.e. interpret the cultural norms).[2]

• Conference call interpretation, as its name indicates, takes place over the phone during a conference call. There is an increasing number of businesses that offer this service.

• Legal or court interpretation can be either consecutive, simultaneous, or whispered interpretation, and can include sight translation as well. Legal interpretation takes place in lawyers' offices and in the courthouse, where interpreters ideally speak in the first person and work in both directions. In Spain, court interpreters (*Traductores jurados*) are certified by the Ministry of Foreign Affairs. In the United States, the Court Interpreter's Act of 1978 entitles those who are hearing impaired or cannot speak English to a certified or otherwise qualified interpreter (at the judiciary's expense) in judicial proceedings instituted by the United States. According to Valero (1995, 99) 95% of federal cases in the United States in need of interpretation are for Spanish speakers. Although in the United States everyone has the right to an interpreter, the certification for interpreters is not adequately legislated across the country. Interesting to note is that the United States legal system does not record statements of defendants in their native tongue, only those spoken by their interpreters. Eades (2003a, 115) explains:

English is the official language of the legal system in countries studied by most of the scholars whose work is drawn on for this review. Further, legal systems in these countries generally assume monolingualism: for example, where interpreters are used in courtrooms, the official transcript records only the English utterances, so that the original utterances, in a language other than English, have no legal status. This means, for example, that in any appeal proceedings the actual utterance of a defendant during trial is unavailable – it is the interpreter's English version which is the basis of any legal argument or decision. Morris (1998) reports a parallel situation with Hebrew in the Israeli legal system, as do Nicholson & Martinsen (1997) with Danish in Denmark.

• Liaison interpretation (also called escort or bilateral interpretation) ocurrs in situations where there are not many people involved, such as business meetings or tourist trips. In contrast to other types of interpretation, liaison interpreters work alone and must do all the interpreting, to and from their LA and LB.
• Sight translation or interpretation is the oral translation of a text as it is read.
• Sign language interpretation is both spoken and signed interpretation and is much better legislated and funded. An important element of sign language interpretation, which some consider transliteration, is that the interpreter must be visible to the audience.
• Whispered interpretation, or chuchotage, consecutive or simultaneous is, as its name indicates, whispered directly to a person or small group.

One problem common to interpretation and translation is the untranslatability of certain words and concepts, but while a translator has time to find the most appropriate equivalent, interpreters must come up with one immediately. As Nolan (2005, 3) explains:

> No translation is ever 'perfect' because cultures and languages differ. However, in practice, the translator is usually held to a higher standard of accuracy and completeness (including the ability to reproduce the style of the original), while the interpreter is expected to convey the essence of the message immediately.

While research is unavoidable in the process of translation, documentation prior to interpretation is invaluable in avoiding untranslatable or unfamiliar terms. Exclusive to interpretation, however, are problems related to the form of communication, especially those related to linguistic distortion.

Audiovisual translation
The demand for audiovisual translation has been growing rapidly, with centers springing up at academic institutions around the world, in great part due to the growth of films as a major source of today's entertainment industry and in part due to globalization. Audiovisual translation involves dubbing, subtitling, surtitling and voiceover, and is one of the areas in translation studies most affected by digitalization and the advent of new technological advances. It is not infrequent nowadays to go to an opera and have the translation via surtitling (or supertitling) on an elongated screen above the stage.

Today films are either dubbed or subtitled, and in the case of DVDs, both. In silent movies there was no need for either: the intertitles were changed for each language and the public imagined the actors were speaking in their language. There were a few films which were actually filmed again in other languages but this practice soon came to a stop because of the high price involved (see the *Dracula* selection in Chapter 8). Dubbing, or revoicing, is the replacement of dialogues in films either in translation or in the original and is done preferably from scripts (sometimes accompanied by notes that clarify jargon), subtitles, or in the worst of cases, it must be done by ear. After the translator translates the dialogue, the script editor modifies the translation and adapts the dialogues. Because translations are always longer than the original, this oftentimes involves shortening them; synchronizing the dialogues to match the mouth movement of the actors is the next step of the script editors.

Dubbing is a cultural preference, although there is some indication that it is preferred in countries with a higher illiteracy rate; and while it is more expensive than subtitling and creates greater changes in the original script than subtitling, most of Latin America, Spain, Italy, France, Germany, Austria and Switzerland are partial to it.[3] The Netherlands, Belgium, Greece, Denmark, Poland, Finland, Sweden Norway and Portugal prefer subtitling. Spain's preference for dubbed movies stems in part from Franco's regime which – anxious to implement Spanish over the other Spanish languages and mindful of the opportunity it afforded censorship, decreed in 1941 that all foreign films were to be subtitled.[4] The law stated:

> Queda prohibida la proyección cinematográfica en otro idioma que no sea el español. . . El doblaje deberá realizarse en estudios españoles que radiquen en el territorio nacional y por personal español.[5]

Spain, France, Italy and Germany subsidize films in their own countries and have protective import quotas in place to guard against the U.S. monopolization of the film (and television) industry. It is interesting to note the high rate of localization in films, or intralanguage dubbing, which is the dubbing of movies in the same language, frequent between the French of France and Quebec and the Spanish of Spain and Latin America. All in all, film critics criticize dubbing for domesticating the source culture of films.

Subtitles, or captions, are the written translation displayed at the bottom of the screen and preferred by some high literacy countries in Europe. It is best for the hearing impaired and, potentially, for language learning. In spite of the fact that subtitling condenses the message and the fact that reading subtitles while looking at the rest of the film is much more tiring and distracting, it is considered to interfere less with the film itself, as the film can be heard in its entirety: music, background noises, voices, intonation and style. Subtitles are considered much less of a domesticating translation technique than dubbing, and are therefore preferred by movie critics. An important advantage to subtitling is the fact that it is a less expensive process than dubbing.

Subtitles have spatial and temporal limitations: they are only on screen between five and seven seconds,[6] only two lines at a time, a maximum of 70 characters with spaces (35 without spaces) per line. Other rules of subtitling include: not starting sentences with numbers, writing out numerals one through nine, attempting to have questions and answers appear at the same time, using dashes for different speakers on the same frame, italics for off-screen voices (e.g. on the phone) or foreign words, upper case for information on signs, and quotation marks on italics for broadcasts or songs. As far as punctuation is concerned, the ellipsis (...) at the end of a frame do not indicate the sentence will continue on the next subtitle but that it is an incomplete thought. However, at the beginning of a phrase on a new frame, the ellipsis means that the dialogue is carried on from the scene before (and therefore the continuing sentence will not begin with upper case). A full stop indicates the end of the reading and tells the viewer s/he can go back to the image. It is important that a subtitler retain the original linguistic structure as much as possible and, to facilitate the reading process, avoid, whenever possible, separating nouns and adjectives from one frame to the next.

Subtitles should accompany the images as closely as possible, a practice which can require condensing messages; some shortening strategies include using apostrophes, making passive sentences active or negative ones positive. The practice is to justify subtitles at the left of the screen in films but in the DVD format to center them, unless it is a dialogue, in which case it is also justified on the left. Often films have different subtitles on the screen and in DVDS (due to a variety of reasons, such as that competing companies put out the different versions). Movies have between 900 and 1000 subtitles while DVDs have 800; TV versions have even fewer, between 700 and 750.[7] Some movies can even have two sets of subtitles in different languages as can be the case in Israel or China. Interestingly, film subtitlers work mainly from scripts but TV subtitlers directly from the videos.

Audiovisual translation also consists of:
• Automated dialogue replacement (ADR) which re-records voices after a scene has been shot and is used for songs (e.g. *Lord of the Rings*) or to censor swear words (e.g. *Die Hard*).
• Live subtitling is for the hearing impaired. It is done by an interpreter who listens to the original and interprets it to a stenographer who then types out the subtitles which appear on screen about two minutes after the original has started. Unfortunately, live subtitling has a high rate of errors. Live subtitling is interlingual interpretation and should not be confused with closed captioning which is also for the hearing impaired but is intralingual interpretation, i.e. a transcription of the original.
• Simulcasts are dubbing over the radio and are used in countries such as South Africa or Thailand.
• Voiceover (VO or V/O) is the placement of voices over images. In documentaries it is not infrequent to hear both the original voice as well as another translated one (the original fading in and out at the beginning and end of the translated voice).

---

1. In ancient Egypt interpreters were considered a professional guild. In the 5th century B.C. Herodotus in *Histories* (Vol. 2, 164) writes: "Now of the Egyptians there are seven classes, and of these one class is called that of the priests, and another that of the

warriors, while the others are the cowherds, swineherds, shopkeepers, interpreters, and boatmen."

2. Attempts are being made across the board to find professionals to substitute natural translators, i.e. the untrained family members, friends or volunteers, especially children for whom family interpretation can be emotionally draining. According to Title VI of the Civil Rights Act of 1964 "No person in the United States shall, on the ground of race, color, or national origin, be excluded from participation in, be denied the benefits of, or be subjected to discrimination under any program or activity receiving Federal financial assistance." Following this directive, President Clinton signed Executive Order 13166 which calls upon agencies receiving federal money to comply with Title VI by making health and human services accessible to everyone, including those with Limited English Proficiency (LEP). This Executive Order has been interpreted as meaning that LEP patients must receive translation services at no cost to them.

3. In some countries where dubbing has been the norm (e.g. Spain) subtitling is increasingly gaining acceptance.

4. Censorship was not officially abolished until 1977, two years after Franco's death.

5. *It is forbidden to show films in any language except Spanish. . . Dubbing must be done in Spanish studios on Spanish territory and by Spanish personnel.*

6. As in written translation, it is important to know the target audience. Adults are fast readers and one-line subtitles should not be on the screen more than 6 seconds (one word lines even less time) as they will tend to reread the line; however, children are slower and therefore need more time to read subtitles.

7. An increasing number of Spanish movies such as Alejandro Amenábar's *Mar adentro* have three sets of subtitles: Spanish for the hearing impaired, Spanish subtitles and English ones.

Chapter 6

The Process of Translation

The process of translation by which a text is transformed from one language to another cannot be fully explained still today. The process for experienced and novice translators includes specifics pertaining to extralinguistic factors, such as identification of the intended reader, the purpose of the text, and, in the case of literary texts, something about the writer. Robinson (2004) writes of the skills and experience that translators develop in their craft, their responsibility to absorb the information in the world around them and also of the role memory plays. Robinson believes that (2004, 50):

> Translation is always an intelligent behavior – even when it seems less conscious and analytical. Translation is a highly complicated process requiring rapid multilayered analyses of semantic fields, syntactic structures, the sociology and psychology of reader- or listener-response, and cultural difference. Like all language use, translation is constantly creative, constantly new. Even translators of the most formulaic source texts, like weather reports, repeatedly face novel situations and must engage in unexpected problem-solving.

The translation process demystified

Ideally, a translator should not start to translate until he or she has read the entire text, paying close attention to the topic, audience, register, style, vocabulary nuances (cognates, collocations, idioms, etc.), and any other extraordinary or recurring characteristic. (If the translator is still a language learner, s/he should pay special attention to verb tenses, conjunctions, direct and indirect complements, and idioms.) The less experienced translator will identify shorter units of translation to translate and the more experienced one, larger units. The more experienced translator will apply translation strategies and techniques unconsciously and the novice translator will have to study the source text, attentive to every aspect of the translation process.

In the process of translation documentation is a vital tool too oftentimes overlooked. Translators need to know how to locate and handle information and use it correctly to make the best translation decisions. A translator's tools include monolingual and bilingual dictionaries, thesaurus, access to specialized dictionaries or data-bases (on-line or in book form) and people. Walter Benjamin's metaphor of the process of translation as a broken vase that needs to be mended is frustrating but documentation is one of the best glues: not only are dictionaries important but so are works by the same author, works on the same topic and the same time period; and, of course, people (acquaintances, friends and family) are an invaluable resource.

The criteria for a correct or incorrect translation can be as wide-ranging as the interpretation of the notion of fidelity or accuracy, or the functional effect of the target text in the target culture. The quality of a translation is guided by 'canons of accuracy,' which are the cultural norms, dictionaries, government agencies, academies, etc. against which translations are measured in the domestic culture (Venuti 1998, 83). Back translation is a common method of assessment used in research, businesses and large organizations such as the World Health Organization to verify the equivalency of the translation. This is a process by which selected passages of the target text are translated back into the source language by a different translator who has not read the ST. The two texts are then compared in order to discover areas of non-equivalence.

Ultimately, target texts benefit from a distancing from their source. Once the translator has finished the translation, s/he should put the ST aside and read the translation to see how it flows. Does it sound like the source language or the target language? Does it make sense?

Common challenges for Spanish-English translators
The more novice translator or the language learner must, in the face of lack of experience, pay close attention to nuances in the shuttle between languages. "The ability to analyze a source text linguistically, culturally, even philosophically or politically is of paramount importance to the translator" (Robinson 2004, 246). In addition, it should not come as a surprise that TT are almost always longer than their ST – presumably, the lack of one-to-one equivalence leads translators to use more words to fill gaps in meaning. This section outlines these and other problem areas that novice Spanish-English translators need to be more aware of.

In the process of translation, the translator must not only choose the most adequate lexical, syntactic, and cultural equivalents, but occasionally the period or time in which to set the new TT. More often than not, the genre of a text is the same in the source language and the target language; however, this is not always the case in poetry where, because of the inherent qualities of poetry such as rhyme, alliteration, or meter, it is not uncommon for poems to be translated into narrative.

Gregory (1980) states that equivalence in register is in itself the single most important factor in the translation process. The notion of register is paramount because language varies according to specific social settings, depending on the subject matter (field), the participants (tenor) and the medium of communication (mode) (Halliday 1978). There are important differences and implications to choosing among options such as *Hey bro!* or *Hello, Mister!* or *Excuse me sir!*

Just as with register, translators must maintain awareness of the type of dialect in a ST and TT, but unlike register, to find a one-to-one dialectal correspondence is more difficult, because "many cultures do not have a dialect which has comparable cultural functions or connotations" (Fawcett 2004, 120). A dialect is a language variety characteristic of a specific group of people; those based on geographic or regional differences are called regionalisms; those based on sociocultural factors are known as sociolects; and idiolects are individual language varieties. When a language or country does not have a written dialect, a sociolect is used in translation instead. Oftentimes, as Berman (2003, 294) points out, "the traditional method of preserving vernaculars is to exoticize them," for example, by a typographical procedure such as italics. Insofar as Spanish and English are concerned, English portrays uneducated speakers via grammatical mistakes while Spanish does so in the accent or dialect.[1]

Formulaic expressions can be translated in two ways: either following the SL or the TL. Vennewitz (1993, 96) speaks of finding counterparts for nursery rhymes, songs, jingles "to set off the same response as the author does in communicating with his reader in his language." Bosch Benítez (2002, 135) explains that the first step in translating this sort of text is to identify its type:

Reconocer la forma o tipo textual a que responde una estructura poética dentro de un cuento supone haber resuelto la mitad del problema, la otra mitad consiste en analizar la función que cumple en el texto.[2]

At the core of the translation process is the notion of textual meaning. Literal meaning is one thing, but as Hervey et al (2001, 98) remind us:

In actual fact, the meaning of a text comprises a number of different layers: referential content, emotional colouring, cultural associations, social and personal connotations, and so on. The many-layered nature of meaning is something translators must never forget.

It follows then that ambiguities (e.g. *I like her painting*) can be frustrating and problematic for novice or experienced translators alike. To resolve ambiguities, both the explicit and the implicit information must be points of reference. A frequent cause of ambiguity is polysemy, which is the condition of words having more than one meaning (e.g. In English *hot* can mean *very warm, spicy,* or *sexy*; in Spanish *hoja* can be from *un árbol, un papel,* or *de afeitar*). In fact, the notion of implicit information is just as difficult to assess because each language has its own world view: English is said to be more objective and impersonal, preferring to highlight manner, while Spanish is said to be more subjective and anarchic and prefers to highlight direction (see Tables 6.1 and 6.2, this chapter). Implicitation implies not translating that which can be understood from the context (e.g. *marble topped tables* > *mesas de mármol*, Valero 1995, 71) however, explicitation is a more universal strategy (Klaudy and Károly 2005).

False friends and cognates are tricky, especially for language learner translators. Cognates are words that look alike and mean the same thing, usually because they have the same origin (e.g. *star - estrella*). False friends, however, are false cognates as they look alike but have a different origin (*haber - have, much - mucho*) or have evolved differently and are different in meaning (e.g. *library - librería, college - colegio, actual - actual, condone - condenar, realize - realizar*). Recognition of collocations is essential for the language learner translator and so is translating collocations in the correct word order in the TL (e.g. *blanco y negro > black and white, safe and sound > sano y salvo*).

Languages vary significantly in the smallest details and translators must be wary of every aspect of the ST. For example, onomatopoeia[3] (*guau*), exclamations (*¡Encima!*), expletives[4] (*¡Mierda!*), stock phrases (*John Doe*), euphemisms[5] (*derrière*), expressions (*to feel blue*), sayings (*El que se pica, ajos come*), formulas (*Sincerely yours*), or forms of address (*Su Ilustrísima*).

When a translator has to translate a known quote, the translator must attempt to look for it and can even resort to inquiring with the writer or the publisher for its origin. Unfortunately, this can take on a treacherous road even with lines as famous as Hamlet's: *To be or not to be, that is the question–* have so many translations: *Ser o no ser, he aquí la cuestión / he ahí la cuestión / he aquí la gran duda / esa es la cuestión / he allí el problema*, etc.

Attention to the work of translators can be gauged by the credit given to them on the cover of books and in reference citations, and fortunately this is becoming more common. When referencing or quoting translations, some scholars advocate adding 'translated' or 'translation' after the page number (e.g. Joyce 1976, 21, translated). In the bibliography, the form of reference depends on the reason for the reference. It is possible to reference the original writer:

Joyce, James (1922/1999) *Ulises*, translation (or, translated by) José María Valverede (1976), Barcelona: Lumen.

or the translator :

Valverde, José María (trans.) (1976/1999) James Joyce, *Ulises*, Barcelona: Lumen.

Names posit a host of particular challenges for translators. Although there is not a fixed strategy for the translation of names, the tendency is to leave them in the original. However, there are many cases when they should or can be translated, unless a foreignizing technique is being applied to the text. The following are some recommendations:
• Many names have an equivalent in the target language (*María - Mary*) but translators may opt for a creative translation, as in children's literature, where meaning, sound and culture can be at odds to each other. Such is the case of J. K. Rowling's *Harry Potter and the Goblet of Fire* (2000) into Spanish, for which the translators (Adolpho Muñoz García and Nieves Martín Azofra) decided on retaining the sound and the English referents of the name of one of the families in the Spanish translation, preferring to lose the original play on words. It is with this decision in mind that *Riddle* becomes *Ryddle*.[6]

• Historical figures, such as kings or saints should be translated when there is an equivalent (*St. James - Santiago*).
• Most professional, religious, military or royal titles have an equivalent (*first lieutenant - teniente*).
• The Pope's name is always translated (*John Paul II – Juan Pablo II*).
• International organisms are usually translated (*United Nations > Naciones Unidas*) while private companies are not (*Burger King* in Spain or *Chupa Chups* in the United States).
• Acronyms and abbreviations are sometimes borrowed into the TL and naturalized; e.g. *la CIA* (but *la Agencia Central de Inteligencia*) or *la FAO* (but *la Organización de las Naciones Unidas para la Agricultura y la Alimentación*). Some abbreviations may not transfer to the TL as abbreviations; such is the case of measurement or name abbreviations (e.g. " (minutes or inches), ' (feet or hours), or *fdo.* (*firmado*).
• There is no fixed formula for translating geographical names but if a street or city is well known and has an equivalent, it is translated (*New York > Nueva York*; *Fifth Avenue > la Quinta Avenida; República Dominicana > Dominican Republic*).
• Plazas or squares are not usually translated (*The Mothers of the Plaza de Mayo*).
• Titles should always be translated, unless they are well known in the source language (in Latin, "Ars poetica" by Horace) to ensure all possible readings. If the title of a book has not been translated, a translator can decide to translate it or not. There are times, however, when some titles might have more than one version, such as Tomás Rivera's *...y no se lo tragó la tierra,* which was first translated as *... And the Earth Did Not Part* by Herminio Ríos and then as *... And the Earth did not Swallow Him* by Evangelina Vigil-Piñón, and is even called at times *... And the Earth Did Not Devour Him.*
• The translation of film titles does not follow clear or specific norms, especially in Spain where in this respect the motivation seems to be less literary than commercial or random. According to Santoyo (1996, 147) "Uno de nuestros vicios nacionales a lo largo de este siglo ha sido el de trastocar los nombres de prácticamente todos los filmes que llegaban de allende de nuestras fronteras."[7] Santoyo (1996, 147-153) lists other tendencies film titles have suffered in translation:

Original title	Creative translation
Bruce Almighty	*Como Dios*
The Sound of Music	*Sonrisas y lágrimas*
Moon over Miami	*Se necesitan maridos*

	Expanded translation
Huckleberry Finn	*Las aventuras de Huckleberry Finn*
Queen Christina	*La reina Cristina de Suecia*

Commercialized translation

Her Friend the Bandit	*Charlot, ladrón elegante*
The Cure	*Charlot en el balneario*

Naturalized translation

Mississippi	*El cantor del río*
Sally, Irene and Mary	*Alma en suplicio*

Romanticized translation

Blossoms in the Dust	*De corazón a corazón*
Night Song	*Mi corazón te guía*
The Best of Everything	*Mujeres frente al amor*

Dramatized translation

Under My Skin	*Venganza del destino*
Sleep, My love	*Pacto tenebroso*
You'll Like My Mother	*Pesadilla en la nieve*

Exaggerated translation

Tarzan and the Amazons	*Tarzán y las intrépidas Amazonas*
The Drum	*Revuelta en la India*

Provocative translation

Model Wife	*Mi mujer no es soltera*
Waltz of the toreadors	*El mayor mujeriego*

Moralizing translation

Let's Make Love	*El multimillonario*
Four Walls	*No hay crimen impune*

Spanish and English contrastive analysis

A contrastive analysis tends to offer greater insight into the underpinnings of language and, by extension, generate constructive guidelines in the translation process. This section provides a look at some of the major differences between English and Spanish, organized into summary tables. Table 6.1 provides an overview of both languages, while Table 6.2 compares discourse and stylistic features. In Tables 6.3 and 6.4, specific grammatical aspects of Spanish and English are contrasted, Table 6.5 looks at questions of differing mechanics and Table 6.1 at domesticating and foreignizing strategies of weights and measurements.

Table 6.1 Spanish – English comparison: general facts

	Spanish	English
Origin	Indo-European, Latin base	Indo-European, Germanic base
Influences	Arabic, German, French, Latin American languages (Nahuatl, Areuco, Quechua, Guaraní)	French Norman
First text	*Glosas Emilianenses*, 11th C.	*Beowulf,* 10th C.
Alphabet	29 letters	26 letters
Diacritic marks	Yes	No (only foreign ones)
Native speakers	5.05% of the world 330 million	4.85% of the world 316 million
World speakers	6.5% 425 million	7.9% 514 million
Authority	Real Academia Española de la Lengua	Noah Webster's Dictionary
Clichés	Ornate, passionate;[8] more suited for the dramatic; explains reality	Plain, factual; more suited for science, business; depicts reality

Table 6.2 Spanish – English comparison: discourse and stylistics

	Spanish	**English**
Point of view	More subjective, anarchic	More objective, impersonal
Discourse	Less dense Formal and informal	Tighter Neutral
Action	Highlights direction	Highlights manner
Word order	SVO (and VSO)[9] Flexible word order	SVO (VSO restricted) Less flexible word order
Syntax	Longer sentences Prefers subordination	Concise, shorter sentences Prefers coordination
Agreement	Number and gender Extensive	Number Limited
Gender	More marked	Less marked
"That"/"Que"	Must be expressed	Hidden
Alliteration[10]	Less use	Greater use
Interjections	Greater use	Less use
Redundancy	Needs greater variation	Accepts little variation
Possession	One form	Two forms
Acronyms	Less use	Greater use
Syllable structure	Polysyllabic	Monosyllabic

Table 6.3 Spanish – English comparison: grammatical aspects I

	Spanish	**English**
Adjectives	Greater syntactic freedom Nouns cannot be adjectives Cannot string adjectives Number and gender markings	Less syntactic freedom Nouns can be adjectives Strings up to 17 adjectives No number or gender markings
Articles	More forms (nine) Less use[11]	Less forms (three) Greater use
Nouns	Greater use of diminutives and augmentatives Number and gender markings	Greater use of prefixes and suffixes Only number markings
Subject pronouns	Optional[12] Five forms for 'you'	Obligatory[13] One form for 'you'
Personal pronouns	14 forms	7 forms
Possessive adjectives	Stressed and unstressed[14] Less use Greater ambiguity	One set Greater use Less ambiguity
Prepositions	20	64
Prepositional Object pronoun	23 forms	13 forms

Table 6.4 Spanish – English comparison: grammatical aspects II

	Spanish	English
Verbs	Two verbs 'ser' and 'estar'	One verb 'to be'
	Less forms	More forms
	Two pasts	One simple past
	Progressive: restricted use, prefers present	Progressive: extremely frequent and versatile
	Future	Modals
	Subjunctive	Gerunds and modals
	12 forms of imperatives	2 forms of imperatives
	Limited use of auxiliaries	Extensive use of auxiliaries
	Single word verbs	Multi-word (phrasal) verbs
	Imperfect	Simple past, past continuous, past perfect continuous, 'used to', 'would'
Number	Prefers singular	Prefers plural
	Prefers cardinals	Prefers ordinals
	Comma separates decimals and the hour	Period separates decimals and the hour

Table 6.5 Spanish – English comparison: format and mechanics

	Spanish	**English**
Upper case	Less use Only the first word and proper names Proper names, words that function as proper names, forms of address, collective nouns[15]	Greater use All words in titles except prepositions and articles Proper names, days of the week, months, nationalities, languages, 'I', titles, forms of address
Punctuation	Sentence link: period or semi-colon Fewer commas Quotation and exclamation marks begin and end sentences Colon introduces new information Letter greeting: a colon Dash introduces dialogue Question and exclamation marks inside dialogue markers Dash ends dialogue only if followed by non-dialogue	Sentence link: period Greater use of commas Commas can replace 'and' Quotation and exclamation marks at the end of sentences Hyphen introduces new information Letter greeting: colon or comma Quotes introduce dialogue Question, exclamation, period and comma inside dialogue markers Quotation marks ends dialogue
Paragraphs	Paragraphs justified	Paragraphs not justified
Contractions	Obligatory	Optional

When translating, it is not the norm to use the exact equivalent of a measurement (e.g. *one yard > 0,914 metros*). Translators either choose a domesticating equivalent (*un metro*) or a more foreignizing one (*una yarda*). Following are some of the major differences with respect to numbers, measurements, distances and weights. Table 6.6 offers possible equivalencies for measurement words in Spanish and English, indicating whether some options are domesticating or foreignizing, if relevant.

Table 6.6 Spanish – English comparison: measurements, distances and weights

Spanish	English *exact*	*domesticating*	*foreignizing*
1 kilómetro	0.621 miles	half a mile	1 kilometer
1 metro	1.093 yards	1 yard	1 meter
1 centímetro	0.394 inches	4 inches	1 centimeter
1 milímetro	0.0394 inches	a fraction of an inch	1 millimeter
1 hectárea	1 hectare	1 acre	1 hectare
1 litro	2.113 pints 1.1 quart	1 gallon	1 liter
1 kilo	2.205 lbs	2 lbs	1 kilo
centígrado	Fahrenheit	Fahrenheit	Centigrade

Spanish	English	*number expression*
millón	million	1,000,000
mil millones	billion	1,000,000,000
billón	trillion	1,000,000,000,000
mil billones	quadrillion	1,000,000,000,000,000
trillón	quintillion	1,000,000,000,000,000,000

---

1. The use of misspellings to indicate a non-standard pronunciation is known as an eye-dialect, while malapropisms misuse similar words, usually with a comical intention (e.g. *physical — fiscal year*).
2. *To recognize the form or type of a poetical structure in a story is to solve half the problem, the other half is solved by analyzing its function in a text.*
3. A number of recent onomatopoeia in Spanish are derived from English comic books because the visual elements supplement comprehension (e.g. what used to be ¡pum! is now ¡bang!).
4. Lunn and Lunsford (2003, 74) note the difficulty of translating swear words, because of regionalisms, equivalence and the 'fashionable' nature which can date them.
5. Euphemisms vary from one region to another and connotations of everyday objects (e.g. fruits and vegetable as to sex organs) can be easily misinterpreted (Child 1992, 66).
6. The Chinese translation is riddled with footnotes explaining British cultural references.

7. *One of our national vices during this century has been to change the titles of practically all the films arriving from abroad.*

8. According to Castro-Paniagua (2000, 28) "Latin culture glorifies emotion over mind, aesthetics over pragmatism."

9. According to Beeby (1996, 253) one way to overcome the difficult subject-verb inversion of Spanish is to start the sentence with 'that'.

10. In English plays on words abound because of the great number of homophones.

11. The use of articles with a first name is derogatory or uneducated, not so with a family name.

12. Munday (2001, 97) remarks on Julio Cortázar's novel *Rayuela* which begins with an unmarked ambiguous *"¿Encontraría a la Maga?"* which can be *"Would I/he/she/it/you find the Magus?"*

13. The oversue of subject pronouns in Spanish is considered an Anglicism.

14. For example, stressed (*mis libros*) and unstressed (*los libros míos*).

15. For example *la Prensa, la Iglesia.*

Chapter 7

Translations into English

TRES TRISTES TIGRES
Guillermo Cabrera Infante

THREE TRAPPED TIGERS
Guillermo Cabrera Infante
Translated from the Cuban by Donald Gardner and
Suzanne Jill Levine in collaboration with the author

Context

Gabriel Cabrera Infante (1929-2005), one of Cuba's foremost literary pens, published *Tres tristes tigres* in 1967, having already exiled himself to Europe. Son of two of the founders of Cuba's Communist Party, Cabrera Infante spent much of his life involved with films; he was the founder of the *Cinemática de Cuba*, the Director of the Cuban Film Institute under Castro and a life-long film critic. In 1997, Cabrera Infante received the prestigious *Premio Cervantes*. In *Three Trapped Tigers,* the author draws a musical picture of Cuba in the 1950s as he celebrates the nightlife of Havana.

Translation

In *The Subversive Scribe* Suzanne Jill Levine offers an unusual glimpse into the process of translation and her intimate collaboration with the author himself. As Levine describes the choices they made translating and the reasons behind them (e.g. the alliteration of the title chosen over meaning), her readers are able to feel the creative literary processes of the writers. For example, how were they to replicate the Cuban Spanish of the novel? (Omitted in the English is a warning that *El libro está en cubano. Es decir, en los diferentes dialectos que se hablan en Cuba.*) After a first attempt at a Cockney version with Donald Gardner, it was decided that the English version should be written in American English "an idiom full of sounds more in tune with crude Cuban than bloody British" (1991, x).

The constant wordplays of this 'open' Joycean novel required an 'open' translation, so much so that revisions were made so that the "original and translation would both be multilingual, both requiring the reader's participation as translator" (1991, 23).

TRES TRISTES TIGRES
Guillermo Cabrera Infante

Showtime! Señoras y señores. *Ladies and gentlemen.* Muy buenas noches, damas y caballeros, tengan todos ustedes. *Good-evening, ladies & gentlemen.* *Tropicana,* el cabaret MÁS fabuloso del mundo... *<<Tropicana>>, the most fabulous night-club in the WORLD...* presenta... *presents...* su *nuevo* espectáculo... *its new show...* en el que artistas de fama continental... *where performers of continental fame...* se encargarán de transportarlos a ustedes al mundo maravilloso... *They will take you all to the wonderful world...* y extraordinario... *of supernatural beauty...* y hermoso... *of the Tropics...* El Trópico para *ustedes* queridos compatriotas... ¡El Trópico en Tropicana! *In the marvelous production of our Rodney the Great...* En la gran, maravillosa producción de nuestro GRANDE, ¡Roderico Neyra!... *<<Going to Brazil>>...* Intitulada, *Me voy pal Brasil...* Taratará tarará, Tatarara tarará taratareo... *Brazuil terra dye nostra felichidade... That was Brezill for you, ladies and gentlemen. That is, my very, very particular version of it!* Brasil, damas y caballeros que me escucháis esta noche. Es decir, *mi* versión del *Brazil* de Carmen Miranda y de Joe *Carioca.* Pero... ¡Brasil, público amable que colma este coliseo del placer y de la alegría y la felicidad! ¡Brasil una vez más y siempre, el Brasil eterno, amables y dignos concurrentes a nuestro forro romano del canto y la danza y el amor a medialuz! *ouh, ouh, ouh. My apologies!...* Público amable, amable público, pueblo de Cuba, la tierra *más* hermosa que ojos humanos vieran, como dijo el Descubridor Colón (no el Colón de Colón, Castillo y Campanario,... Jojojó. Sino ¡Cristóbal Colón, el de las carabelas!)... Pueblo, público, queridos concurrentes, perdonen un momento mientras me dirijo, en el idioma de *Chakespeare,* en *English,* me dirijo a la selecta concurrencia que colma *todas y cada unas* de las localidades de este emporio del amor y la vida risueña. Quiero hablarle, si la amabilidad proverbial del Respetable cubano me lo permite, a nuestra ENorme concurrencia americana: caballerosos y radiantes turistas que visitan la tierra de las *gay senyoritaes and brave caballerros...*

THREE TRAPPED TIGERS
Guillermo Cabrera Infante
Translated from the Cuban by Donald Gardner and Suzanne Jill Levine in collaboration with the author

Showtime! *Señoras y señores*. Ladies and gentlemen. And a very good evening to you all, ladies and gentlelmen. *Muy buenas noches, damas y caballeros*. Tropicana! the MOST fabulous nightclub in the WORLD–*el cabaret MAS fabuloso del mundo*–presents–*presenta*–its latest show–*su nuevo espectáculo*–where performers of Continental fame will take you all to the wonderful world of supernatural beauty of the Tropics–*al mundo maravilloso y extraordinario y hermoso*: The Tropic in the Tropicana! *El Trópico en Tropicana!* In the marvelous production of our Rodney the Great–*el gran Roderico Neyra*–entitled *Me voy pal Brasil*–that means "Going to Brazil."... *Brazuil terra dye nostra felichidade*. That was Brezill for you, ladies and gentlemen, in Brassilian! *El Brasil brasileiro, damas y caballeros que me escucháis esta noche*. That is my very, very particular version of it! *Es decir, mi version del Brazil de Carmen Miranda y de Joe Carioca*–Brasil, the land of Carmen Miranda and Joe Carioca. But–*Pero*–Brazil, dear public assembled here in this coliseum of pleasure and gaiety and happiness! *Brasil una vez más y siempre*–Brazil once and for always, eternal Brazil, honorable and dear visitors to our Romance Forum of song and dance and love by candlelight!! ouh, ouh, ouh! ooh! la! la! My apologies! . . . *Público amable, amable público, pueblo de Cuba, la tierra MAS hermosa que ojos humanos vieran, como dijo el Descubridor Colón (eso es, el colon de las carabelas– ho ho ho!)* . . . *Pueblo, público, queridos concurrentes, perdonen un momento mientras me dirijo a la selecta concurrencia que colma todas y cada unas de las localidades de este emporio del amor y la vida risueña. Quiero hablarles, si la amabilidad proverbial del Respetable cubano me lo permite, a los caballerosos y radiantes turistas que visitan nuestra tierra*–to our ENORMOUS American audience of glamorous and distinguished tourists who are visiting the land of the gay senyoritas and brave caballerros . . .

VERSOS SENCILLOS
José Martí

SIMPLE VERSES
José Martí
Translations Manuel A. Tellechea and Anne Fountain

Context

Born in Havana to Spanish parents in 1853, José Martí would become Cuba's national hero in his quest for national independence, both from Spanish colonial rule and brewing U.S. annexation. Exiled as a teenager, Martí spent the rest of his life in Europe, the United States and Latin America writing poetry and political and philosophical essays. Regarded by many as the father of Spanish modernist poetry, Martí died on one of his rare trips to Cuba, in the battle of Dos Ríos in 1895. Many are unaware that the well-known song "Guantanamera" is in fact an adaptation of Martí's "Verso I" by Julián Orbón (music by José Fernández Díaz).

Translation

Without a doubt, poetry is one of the most difficult genres to translate. Rhyme, rhythm or meter (beat pattern, number of syllables), meaning, form, imagery, metaphor, sound, tone or mood cannot all be replicated into the target language. Due to the nature of the genre, translators of poetry are thrust head onto the dilemma of content versus form from the moment they decide to take on a translation of a poem. The two English versions presented here by Anne Fountain and Manuel Tellechea prove how even contemporary translations, while adhering to some of the formal characteristics of Martí's poetry such as the ABAB rhyme, can vary so significantly.

VERSOS SENCILLOS I
José Martí

Yo soy un hombre sincero
De donde crece la palma,
Y antes de morirme quiero
Echar mis versos del alma.

Yo vengo de todas partes,
Y hacia todas partes voy:
Arte soy entre las artes,
En los montes, monte soy.

Yo sé los nombres extraños
De las yerbas y las flores,
Y de mortales engaños,
Y de sublimes dolores.

Yo he visto en la noche oscura
Llover sobre mi cabeza
Los rayos de lumbre pura
De la divina belleza.

Alas nacer vi en los hombros
De las mujeres hermosas:
Y salir de los escombros,
Volando las mariposas.

He visto vivir a un hombre
Con el puñal al costado,
Sin decir jamás el nombre
De aquella que lo ha matado.

Rápida, como un reflejo,
Dos veces vi el alma, dos:
Cuando murió el pobre viejo,
Cuando ella me dijo adiós.

Temblé una vez —en la reja,
A la entrada de la viña,—
Cuando la bárbara abeja
Picó en la frente a mi niña.

Gocé una vez, de tal suerte
Que gocé cual nunca:—cuando
La sentencia de mi muerte
Leyó el alcaide llorando.

Oigo un suspiro, a través
De las tierras y la mar,
Y no es un suspiro,—es
Que mi hijo va a despertar.

Si dicen que del joyero
Tome la joya mejor,
Tomo a un amigo sincero
Y pongo a un lado el amor.

Yo he visto al águila herida
Volar al azul sereno,
Y morir en su guarida
La víbora del veneno.

Yo sé bien que cuando el mundo
Cede, lívido, al descanso,
Sobre el silencio profundo
Murmura el arroyo manso.

Yo he puesto la mano osada,
De horror y júbilo yerta,
Sobre la estrella apagada
Que cayó frente a mi puerta.

Oculto en mi pecho bravo
La pena que me lo hiere:
El hijo de un pueblo esclavo
Vive por él, calla, y muere.

Todo es hermoso y constante,
Todo es música y razón,
Y todo, como el diamante,
Antes que luz es carbón.

Yo sé que el necio se entierra
Con gran lujo y con gran llanto,-
Y que no hay fruta en la tierra
Como la del camposanto.

Callo, y entiendo, y me quito
La pompa del rimador:
Cuelgo de un árbol marchito
Mi muceta de doctor.

SIMPLE VERSES I
José Martí
Translation Manuel A. Tellechea

A sincere man am I
From the land where palm trees grow,
And I want before I die
My soul's verses to bestow.

I'm a traveler to all parts,
And a newcomer to none:
I am art among the arts,
With the mountains I am one.

I know the strange names of willows,
And can tell flowers with skill:
I know of lies that can kill,
And I know of sublime sorrows.

I have seen through dead of night
Upon my head softly fall,
Rays formed of the purest light
From beauty celestial.

! have seen wings that were surging
From beautiful women's shoulders,
And seen butterflies emerging
From the refuse heap that moulders.

I have known a man to live
With a dagger at his side,
And never once the name give
Of she by whose hand he died.

Twice, for an instant, did I
My soul's reflection descried,
Twice: when my poor father died
And when she bade me good-bye.

I trembled once, when I flung
The vineyard gate, and to my dread,
The dastard hornet had stung
My little girl on the forehead.

Such great luck to me once came
As no man would dare to envy
When in tears my jailer read me
The death warrant with my name.

I hear a sigh across the earth,
I hear a sigh over the deep:
It is no sign reaching my hearth,
But my son waking from sleep.

If they say I have obtained
The pick of the jeweller's trove,
A good friend is all I've gained
And I have put aside love.

I have seen an eagle gliding,
Though wounded, across the skies;
I know the cubby where lies
The snake of its venom dying.

I know that the world is weak
And must soon fall to the ground,
And then, midst the quiet profound
The gentle brook will speak.

While trembling with joy and dread,
I have touched with hand so bold
A once-bright star that fell dead
From heaven at my threshold.

I have hid in my brave heart
The most terrible of pains,
The son of a land in chains,
Lives for it and dies apart.

All is beautiful and right,
All is as music and reason;
And as diamonds ere their season,
All is coal before it's light.

I know when fools are laid to rest
Honor and tears will abound,
And that of all fruits, the best
Is left to rot in holy ground.

Without a word, I've understood
And put aside the pompous muse;
From a withered branch, I choose
To hang my doctoral hood.

VERSOS SENCILLOS I
José Martí
Translation Anne Fountain

A sincere man am I
Born where the palm trees grow,
And long before I die
My soul's verses to bestow.

No boundaries bind my heart
I belong to every land:
I am art among art,
A peak among peaks I stand.

I know the exotic names
Of every flower and leaf.
I know of betrayal's claims
And I know of exalted grief.

I've seen how beauteous streams
Flow through the dark of night
And descend as radiant beams
In a luminous shower of light.

As if by wings set free,
I've seen women's shoulders rise:
And beauty emerge from debris
In a flight of butterflies.

I've seen a man live with pain
The dagger wounds at his side,
Yet never reveal the name
Of her by whose hand he died.

Two times I've sensed inside
The soul's reflection go by.
Once when my father died
And once when she bade goodbye.

Once I trembled with fear
Close by the arbor's vine,
As an angry bee drew near
To sting a child of mine.

That day of my death decree
I felt triumph and pride,
For the warden who read it to me
Pronounced the sentence and cried.

Beneath me I hear a sigh
From the slumber of earth and sea.
But in truth it's the morning cry
Of my son who awakens me.

The jewel esteemed the most?
The value I most revere?
I would of friendship boast
And hold not love so dear.

The wounded eagle, I know
Can soar to the bluest skies
While the venomous viper below
Chokes on its poison and dies.

I know that when life must yield
And leave us to restful dreams
That alongside the silent field
Is the murmur of gentle streams.

To sorrows and joy, I reply
By placing a loyal hand,
On the star that refused to die –
Proud symbol of my land.

My heart holds anguish and pains
From a wound which festers and cries
The son of a people in chains
Lives for them, hushes and dies.

All is lovely and right
All is reason and song
Before the diamond is bright
Its night of carbon is long.

I know that the foolish may die
With burial pomp and tears
And that no land can supply
The fruit which the graveyard bears.

Silent, I quit the renown
And boast of a poet's rhyme
And rest my doctoral gown
On a tree withered with time.

...Y NO SE LO TRAGÓ LA TIERRA
Tomás Rivera

...AND THE EARTH DID NOT DEVOUR HIM
Tomás Rivera
Translated by Evangelina Vigil-Piñon

Context

Tomás Rivera was born into a Chicano migrant family in 1935 and went on to become a renowned writer, poet and college chancellor. His works, which deal with the plight of the Mexican American, spearheaded the expansion of the American literary canon and forefronted the then nascent U.S. Latino literature. In the seminal *...y no se lo tragó su familia* (*...And the Earth Did Not Devour Him*), Rivera portrays the resilience of Chicano children as they confront tradition, socioeconomic hardship and the condition of being Mexican American.

Translation

These opening lines of *...y no se lo tragó la tierra* beckon the reader to discover who 'he' is and why the earth did not part – an ambitious and ambiguous endeavor presented in seemingly simple Spanish. The translator Evangelina Vigil-Piñón follows the original Spanish as closely as possible, choosing though the shorter sentences of English. Comparing the previous translation by Herminio Ríos, it is seems she follows him closely as well, down to the omission of a complete sentence. Having said this– should translators give credit to those that preceded them?

...Y NO SE LO TRAGÓ LA TIERRA
Tomás Rivera

El año perdido

Aquel año se le perdió. A veces trataba de recordar y ya para cuando creía que se estaba aclarando todo un poco se le perdían las palabras. Casi siempre empezaba con un sueño donde despertaba de pronto y luego se daba cuenta de que realmente estaba dormido. Luego ya no supo si lo que pensaba había pasado o no.

Siempre empezaba todo cuando oía que alguien le llamaba por su nombre pero cuando volteaba la cabeza a ver quién era el que le llamaba, daba una vuelta entera y así quedaba donde mismo. Por eso nunca podía acertar ni quién le llamaba ni por qué, y luego hasta se le olvidaba el nombre que le habían llamado. Pero sabía que él era a quien llamaban.

Una vez se detuvo antes de dar la vuelta entera y le entró miedo. Se dio cuenta de que él mismo se había llamado. Y así empezó el año perdido.

Trataba de acertar cuándo había empezado aquel tiempo que había llegado a llamar año. Se dio cuenta de que siempre pensaba que pensaba y de allí no podía salir. Luego se ponía a pensar en que nunca pensaba y era cuando se le volvía todo blanco y se quedaba dormido. Pero antes de dormirse veía y oía muchas cosas. . .

...AND THE EARTH DID NOT DEVOUR HIM
Tomás Rivera
Translated by Evangelina Vigil-Piñon

The Lost Year

That year was lost to him. At times he tried to remember, and just about when he thought everything was clearing up some, he would be at a loss for words. It almost always began with a dream in which he would suddenly awaken and then realize that he was really asleep. Then he wouldn't know whether what he was thinking had happened or not.

It always began when he would hear someone calling him by his name but when he turned his head to see who was calling, he would make a complete turn and there he would end-up in the same place. This was why he never could discover who was calling him nor why. And then he even forgot the name he had been called.

One time he stopped at mid-turn and fear suddenly set in. He realized that he had called himself. And thus the lost year began.

He tried to figure out when that time he had come to call "year" had started. He became aware that he was always thinking and thinking and from this there was no way out. Then he started thinking about how he never thought and this was when his mind would go blank and he would fall asleep. But before falling asleep he saw and heard many things...

RIMA XXI
Gustavo Adolfo Bécquer

RHYME XXI
Gustavo Adolfo Bécquer
Translations Owen Innsly, Jules Renard, Young Allison, Rupert Craft-Cooke, Henry Sullivan and David F. Altabe

Context

Gustavo Adolfo Bécquer (1836-70) is without a doubt the most famous Romantic poet in Spanish. After his untimely death at age 34, Bécquer's friends gathered his brief poems in what is known as *Rimas*. In his *Rimas* and *Leyendas*, readers are swept into his ideal of love, aesthetics, and the melancholy of misfortune in love.

Translation

Bécquer's musical poetry, which revives popular poetry with modern techniques, can be described as simple for its sparse use of adjectives and verbs. Sullivan, the most contemporary of the translators of "Rima XXI" included here, explains in his Translator's Introduction that while the choice of meter or rhythm according to English poetic tradition was borne of tradition (hendecasyllable > iambic pentameter), his choice of words was more difficult. According to Sullivan, while the brevity of monosyllabic English can easily capture the polysyllabic meter of Spanish, he has preferred to use longer words in English to transpose the tone (more emotional and archaic) that one would expect of Bécquer's Victorian contemporaries.

The following six translations are ordered chronologically, from oldest to most contemporary.

RIMA XXI
Gustavo Adolfo Bécquer

¿Qué es poesía? –dices mientras clavas
    en mi pupila tu pupila azul.
¿Qué es poesía? ¿Y tú me lo preguntas
    Poesía. . . eres tú.

RHYME XXI
Gustavo Adolfo Bécquer
Translation Owen Innsly

What is poetry? thou say'st, and meanwhile fixest
On mine eye thine eye of deepest blue;
What is poetry? And canst thou ask it?
    Why, - poetry - is - thou!

RHYME XXI
Gustavo Adolfo Bécquer
Translation Jules Renard

"What is poesy," you ask
While you fix your pupil blue
On my own. - An easy task
To reply; but why should you
Put this question unto me?
    −You, yourself, are poesy.

RHYME XXI
Gustavo Adolfo Bécquer
Translation Young Allison

"What is poesy?" you ask me, gazing
Into mine eyes with your eyes blue.
What is poesy? And do you truly ask me?
    Poesy . . . ARE???? you.

RHYME XXI
Gustavo Adolfo Bécquer
Translation Rupert Craft-Cooke

"What is poetry?" you ask, as you hold
My eyes with your eyes of blue;
"What is poetry? Well, since you ask me,
    It's you."

RHYME XXI
Gustavo Adolfo Bécquer
Translation David F. Altabe

"What is poetry?" you ask,
Gazing at me with eyes so blue,
And it is you, you who ask me?
Poetry. . . why, it is you.

RHYME XXI
Gustavo Adolfo Bécquer
Translation Henry Sullivan

"What is poetry?" you say while fixing
    your azure pupil on my eye.
"What is poetry? And you ask me?
    Poetry. . . is you!."

CUENTOS DE HADAS Y ALGO MÁS
Marjorie Agosín

FAIRY TALES AND SOMETHING MORE
Marjorie Agosín
Translation Cola Franzen

Context
Born in the United States and raised in Chile, Marjorie Agosín left Chile with her parents following General Pinochet's coup in 1973. Poet, critic, human activist and spokesperson for women from the Third World, Agosín's first collection of poems to appear in translation, *Brujas y algo más / Witches and Other Things*, explores the theme of women through male tropes.

Translation
In "Cuentos de hadas y algo más" Marjorie Agosín makes use of fairy tales to direct her readers' attention to the lives of 'real' women as they compare to the female models represented in them. Because exact equivalence in poetry is so elusive, the stress in the opening lines of the two versions shifts from the 'positive' female role model to the derision of male attributes. The simple Spanish is not difficult to replicate in English (including alliteration); however, it is the formulaic expression at the end of all fairy tales in Spanish –*colorín colorado [este cuento] se ha acabado*– which the translator Cola Franzen expertly handles.

CUENTOS DE HADAS Y ALGO MÁS
Marjorie Agosín

A Blanca Nieves los enanos
no la tuvieron de adorno
hacía sus deberes
hilaba calcetines
y quién sabe
como terminarían sus noches
en un cuarto de siete precoces señores,
La Cenicienta cenizas,
tampoco muy bien la pasó
limpiando la ropa de los otros,
descalza perpetua
hasta que un caballero
de ella se apiadó
y un zapato parece que le dió
el zapato bien le quedó
y esa otra cosa también cupo.
La Caperucita Roja
tuvo que dormir con un lobo
pero todas nosotras
hemos dormido con lobos que roncan
y nos amenazan con el cielo y la tierra
con días felices recogiendo
cabellos del lavabo
trayendo café y periódico
como amaestradas amas de amos.
Y los cuentos de hadas
colorín colorado
hasta ahora nunca se han acabado.

FAIRY TALES AND SOMETHING MORE
Marjorie Agosín
Translation Cola Franzen

The dwarves didn't keep
Snow White as an ornament
she did her chores
mended socks
and who knows
how she ended her nights
in a room with seven precocious fellows
Cinderella cinders,
also no very easy road
washing other people's clothes
always barefoot
until a gentleman
took pity on her
and it seems he gave her one shoe
and the shoe fit her very well
and the other thing fit also.
Little Red Riding Hood
had to sleep with a wolf
but all of us women
have slept with wolves that snore
and promise us heaven and earth
happy days gathering up
hair from the washbasin
fetching coffee and the newspaper
as tamed mistresses of masters
and the Fairy Tales
rose-colored off-colored
have never had any ever after

EL NEGOCIO DE INVENTAR NOMBRES
Antonio Jiménez Barca

HALLOWED BE THY BRAND NAME
Antonio J. Barca

Context

This article appeared in the leading Spanish newspaper *El País* on June 18th, 2006 and in its translated version in *El País – English Edition* two days later. "El negocio de inventar nombres" is an example of journalistic writing: colloquial, rapid paced, with sparse adjectival ornamentation, and embedded with frequent quotes.

Translation

The evolution of "El negocio de inventar nombres" to "Hallowed be thy brand name" is representative of the transformations involved in journalistic translations. This article, originally published in the Sunday magazine of *El País*, was shortened –contrary to what could be said to be the norm in translation in general– to fit the daily English edition and paragraph indentation needed to conform to the visual realities of narrower columns. As is the case so many times, the translator of the article is not mentioned, although she (or he) has obviously taken great care with the translation, following conventions of punctuation. style and register. Even the small error at the beginning of the piece (or did the translator know something the writer of the original piece did not?) is indicative of what can happen in translation due to countless factors, usually haste. It is interesting to note that the English editors of *El País* do not seem to be aware of the order of surnames in Spanish.

EL NEGOCIO DE INVENTAR NOMBRES
Antonio Jiménez Barca

A Fernando Beltrán le contrataron hace años porque a un sitio recién inaugurado no iba nadie. Ni familias, ni niños, ni turistas, ni nadie. "Se llamaba Parque Biológico de Madrid y sus responsables decían que o empezaba a ir gente o cerraban en unos meses. Yo acudí temiéndome lo peor: me imaginaba un lugar aburrido... Y resulta que allí había una casa llena de mariposas, un Polo Norte en miniatura con pingüinos de verdad, una miniselva con monos... ¡Era estupendo! Claro que ¿qué padre lleva a su niño pequeño a algo llamado Parque Biológico de Madrid? El nombre fallaba, sin duda. Así que me puse a trabajar. Y les propuse el que tiene ahora: Faunia. Ahora va más gente. No han cerrado".

Fernando Beltrán, de 50 años, es poeta. Ha publicado más de una decena de libros. Una antología de sus poemas ha sido traducida al francés. Su último trabajo, *El corazón no muere,* acaba de salir en Hiperión. Y como todo buen poeta, ha vivido siempre de otra cosa. Fue administrativo, librero, periodista, actor, guionista de cine y empleado en una agencia de publicidad. En nada duró mucho. Pero en el mundo de la publicidad vislumbró su hueco: "No se les daba importancia a los nombres. Ni siquiera tenían mucho presupuesto para eso. Para el *marketing,* sí; para el logotipo de la marca en cuestión, también, y para el mercado, pero el nombre era lo de menos". Beltrán decidió, hace 14 años, crear una empresa dedicada exclusivamente a la creación de nombres. Sus amigos le dijeron que si estaba loco, que se iba a morir de hambre, que para eso, mejor dedicarse en exclusiva a la poesía...

Algo difícil y caro

No se ha muerto de hambre. Al contrario. La industria de buscar el nombre exacto para nuevas empresas, o nuevos productos de empresas conocidas, ha cobrado cada vez más importancia en la publicidad. En Estados Unidos, al fenómeno se le denomina *naming,* y hay empresas de cientos de empleados dedicadas casi en exclusiva a la búsqueda de la designación exacta de cada cosa. Es algo difícil...y caro. "Hay muchos precios, claro. Y hay muchos factores que influyen en la factura final", comenta Gonzalo Brujó, consejero delegado de Interbrand-España, una compañía internacional que crea marcas, con más de 1.200 empleados en todo el mundo y 40 delegaciones repartidas por el planeta. "Pero el precio puede ir desde los 12.000 euros para el nombre de una pequeña empresa hasta los 70.000 para la denominación de un coche estrella de una firma mundialmente conocida, como Ford Mondeo, por ejemplo, que lo hicimos nosotros, en España", comenta Brujó.

A Beltrán le costó lo suyo aguantar. "Yo trabajaba solo, al principio hasta tenía que ocultar a algún director de empresa que yo era el único miembro de mi empresa, o que era poeta, porque no sonaba demasiado serio, o citarle en vestíbulos de hotel, porque me daba un poco de apuro quedar en la habitación del piso alquilado donde instalé la oficina. Mis amigos me decían que lo dejara, pero yo aguanté... y entonces vino lo de Amena, y me salvé", recuerda.

HALLOWED BE THY BRAND NAME
Antonio J. Barca
Translator unknown

Five years ago Fernando Beltrán was hired because a business had just been inaugurated, but nobody was turning up – no families, no children, no tourists." It was called the Madrid Biological Park, and the people running it told me that if people didn't start coming to it they would close in a few months."
I went there fearing the worst, something dreadfully boring. And it turned out there was a house filled with butterflies, a miniature North Pole with real penguins, a mini-jungle with monkeys. It was wonderful. But what parent would take a small child to something called the Madrid Biological Park? What it wanted was a name. So I went to work and proposed Faunia, which is what it is now called. Now more people go there. It hasn't closed."

Fernando Beltrán, 50, is a poet with more than a dozen books to his name. An anthology of his poems has been translated into French. His latest work, *El corazón no muere* (The heart does not die), has just been published by Hiperión. Like most poets, he has always done something else for a living – office worker, bookseller, journalist, actor, scriptwriter, advertising copywriter. No job lasted long. But in the advertising world, he saw a niche: "Nobody seemed to care about names. There wasn't even much of a budget for them. Marketing and logos got a lot of attention, but the name was the least of considerations."

So 14 years ago, Beltrán decided to create a firm exclusively for the creation of names. His friends thought that he was crazy; since he was going to starve anyway, they thought he might as well devote all his time to poetry.

But he hasn't starved – quite the contrary. The demand for exactly the right name for new businesses and products has bloomed. In the United States, the phenomenon is called naming, and there are firms with hundreds of employees working on it. It is often difficult, and expensive. "There are many prices, of course, and factors that go into the final bill," says Gonzalo Brujó, of the Spanish subsidiary of Interbrand, a firm with 1200 employees and 40 offices worldwide, which creates brand names. "The price can range from €12.000 for a small company to €70.000 for a new car model from a global firm – such as Ford Mondeo, which we invented in Spain."

For Beltrán it was hard to keep going at first. He often met prospective clients in hotel lobbies so as not to show them his diminutive office, or reveal he was the only person in his firm. "But then Amena came along, and saved me."

ESTRUCTURAS INTERNAS, ESTRUCTURAS EXTERNAS Y TRADUCCIÓN
Humberto López Morales

DEEP STRUCTURE, SURFACE STRUCTURE AND TRANSALTION
Humberto López Morales
Translation María Esther Castro

Context
"Estructuras internas, estructuras externas y traducción" by Prof. Humberto López Morales appeared in 1982 in a book entitled *Problemas de la traducción / Problems in Translation*. This article by the famed linguist, member, president and ex-president of different linguistic societies, such as the Sociedad Lingüística del Caribe, appears alongside a collection of essays dealing with translation studies from a multiple range of perspectives.

Translation
"Estructuras internas, estructuras externas y traducción" is an academic essay on the semantic and linguistic nature of translation and the "expressive burdens" of transferring linguistic forms to the TL because "the single deep structure may have various surface forms" as López Morales indicates at the end of his paper. The difficulty of this specific translation resides, on the one hand, in the scholarly vocabulary and, on the other, in the sophisticated and erudite vocabulary of a formal register that cannot always be found in the more neutral English register.

ESTRUCTURAS INTERNAS, ESTRUCTURAS EXTERNAS Y TRADUCCIÓN
Humberto López Morales

Son dos los problemas básicos que durante mucho tiempo han mantenido el divorcio entre lingüística y traducción. Por una parte, el rechazo de varias escuelas de lingüística a considerar la semántica dentro de las fronteras de su ciencia; por otra, la condena de múltiples traductores que relegan el papel lingüístico en su ejercicio a un mínimo intrascendente.

El primero de los puntos es de importancia sobresaliente, pues por mucho que se afine y enriquezca la descripción de una operación traductora, la sustancia semántica quedará siempre como elemento axial en la búsqueda de equivalentes formales. La traducción no pudo ser trabajada con instrumental lingüístico desde ninguna de las posiciones de los formalistas postbloomfieldianos, sencillamente porque su 'antimentalismo' los llevó a levantar un muro infranqueable entre elementos de lengua y elementos ajenos; entre estos últimos quedaba situado el significado del signo. En teoría al menos, el rigor y la objetividad del análisis de los enunciados sólo les permitió la manipulación de formas: análisis componencial y confección de cuadros de distribución.

El rechazo de la semántica como objeto de estudio de la lingüística no fue – como se sabe– exclusivo del estructuralismo formalista norteamericano. Hjelmslev no fue menos tajante en su postura, pues dio orden de desahucio contra toda sustancia lingüística y no sólo la del contenido. Hay que añadir a esta rápida nómina, varias tendencia del funcionalismo europeo que, aunque en diverso grado, utilizaban los contenidos semánticos como apoyaturas analíticas y no como material de análisis.

DEEP STRUCTURE, SURFACE STRUCTURE AND TRANSALTION
Humberto López Morales
Translation María Esther Castro

There are two basic problems that have kept the division between linguistics and translation open. On the one hand, various schools of linguistics have been reluctant to consider semantics within the bounds of the science, and, or the other hand, many translators have relegated the linguistic aspect of their work to a minimal role.

The first of these aspects is of special importance, because no matter how much the description of a translation is polished and enriched, the semantic substance will remain an essential element in the search for formal equivalents. Translation could not be worked with linguistic tools from any of the viewpoints of post-Bloomfieldian formalists simply because their "antimentalism" made them erect an insurmountable wall between linguistic and non-linguistic elements; among the latter was included the meaning of the sign. Theoretically at least, rigor and objectivity in the analysis of the spoken language allowed only for the handling of forms: constituent analysis and the preparation tables of distribution.

The rejection of semantics as an object of study for linguists was not –of course– only characteristic of North American formalist structuralism. Hjelmslev was just as sharp in his position when he ruled out all linguistic substance and not only that of content. To this brief list must be added the various tendencies of European functionalism that used, although to a different degree, semantic content as an analytical tool and not as material for analysis.

Chapter 8

Translations into Spanish

LIFE & TIMES OF MICHAEL K
J.M. Coetzee

VIDA Y ÉPOCA DE MICHAEL K
J.M. Coetzee
Translations Concha Manella

Context

Life and Times of Michael K is J.M. Coetzee's fourth novel. Born in South Africa in 1940, Coetzee writes generally of South Africa although not specifically of the racial issues or tensions the country suffered during apartheid. Considered by some critics to be a postmodernist writer, J. M. Coetzee won the Nobel Prize for literature in 2003.

Translation

J. M. Coetzee is considered a sparse and precise writer. The conciseness of the short phrases of *Life and Times of Michael K,* based on part on his widespread use of verbs and prepositions, is not available to Spanish and therefore requires frequent paraphrasing. The vocabulary does not pose extreme problems although, while not especially difficult, it can be sophisticated and specific; the fact that the names in the translation remain unchanged follows a foreignizing trend in this area.

It is not often that translators are able to revise their translations; the two versions of *Life and Times of Michael K* by the same translator (1987 and 2006) offer an insight into the process. Small mistakes are corrected (e.g. pronouns), vocabulary is honed (e.g. *advirtió* vs. *vio*), different choices are made (e.g. *desesperándose* vs. *impacientándose*), but more importantly the revisions seen here show how the translator has conformed the translation to a more 'natural' Spanish by revising the syntax (word order), grammatical forms (e.g. preterite vs. -ing) and the lexicon (*bebé* vs. *lactante*).

LIFE & TIMES OF MICHAEL K
J.M. Coetzee

The first thing the midwife noticed about Michael K when she helped him out of his mother into the world was that he had a hare lip. The lip curled like a snail's foot, the left nostril gaped. Obscuring the child for a moment from its mother, she prodded open the tiny bud of a mouth and was thankful to find the palate whole.

To the mother she said: 'You should be happy, they bring luck to the household.' But from the first Anna K did not like the mouth that would not close and the living pink flesh it bared to her. She shivered to think of what had been growing in her all these months. The child could not suck from the breast and cried with hunger. She tried a bottle; when it could not suck from the bottle she fed it with a teaspoon, fretting with impatience when it coughed and spluttered and cried.

'It will close up as he grows older,' the midwife promised. However, the lip did not close, or did not close enough, nor did the nose come straight.

She took the child with her to work and continued to take it when it was no longer a baby. Because their smiles and whispers hurt her, she kept it away from other children. Year after year Michael K sat on a blanket watching his mother polish other people's floors, learning to be quiet.

VIDA Y ÉPOCA DE MICHAEL K
J.M. Coetzee
Translation Concha Manella

Lo primero que la comadrona vio de Michael K al ayudarle a salir de su madre y entrar en el mundo fue su labio leporino. El labio se enroscaba como un caracol, el orificio nasal izquierdo se entreabría. Ocultando el niño a su madre durante un momento, abrió con la punta de los dedos el diminuto brote de boca y dio gracias al ver el paladar completo.

A la madre le dijo:

–Debe alegrarse, traen suerte al hogar. –Pero desde el primer momento a Anna K le disgustó esa boca que no se cerraba mostrándole un trozo de carne viva. Se estremeció al pensar lo que en todos esos meses había estado creciendo en ella. El niño no podía mamar y lloraba de hambre. Ella intentaba alimentarle con biberón, y cuando tampoco podía succionar del biberón, le alimentaba con una cucharita, impacientándose cuando el niño tosía, regurgitaba y lloraba.

–Se cerrará cuando crezca –prometió la comadrona. Sin embargo, el labio no se cerró, o al menos totalmente, y la nariz tampoco se enderezó.

Llevaba al niño con ella al trabajo y siguió haciéndolo incluso cuando ya no era un lactante. Le mantuvo alejado de otros niños porque sus risitas y susurros la herían. Año tras año Michael K se sentaba en una manta viendo a su madre encerar los suelos de otros, aprendiendo a callar.

VIDA Y ÉPOCA DE MICHAEL K
J.M. Coetzee
Revised translation Concha Manella

Lo primero que advirtió la comadrona en Michael K cuando lo ayudó a salir del vientre de su madre y entrar en el mundo fue su labio leporino. El labio se enroscaba como un caracol, la aleta izquierda de la nariz estaba entreabierta. Le ocultó el niño a la madre durante un instante, abrió la boca diminuta con la punta de los dedos, y dio gracias al ver el paladar completo.

A la madre le dijo:

—Debería alegrarse, traen suerte al hogar.

Pero desde el primer momento a Anna K le disgustó esa boca que no se cerraba, mostrándole un trozo de carne viva. Se estremeció al pensar lo que había crecido en ella todos esos meses. El niño no podía mamar y lloraba de hambre. Trató de alimentarlo con biberón, pero como él tampoco podía tirar de la tetina, le daba de comer con una cucharita, desesperándose cuando el niño se atragantaba, devolvía y lloraba.

—Se cerrará cuando crezca —le aseguró la comadrona.

Sin embargo, el labio no se cerró, o al menos no lo suficiente, y la nariz tampoco se corrigió.

Llevó al niño con ella al trabajo, y siguió llevándolo incluso cuando ya no era un bebé. Lo mantuvo alejado de los otros niños porque sus risitas y susurros la herían. Año tras año, Michael K, sentado en una manta, contempló a su madre encerar los suelos de otros, y aprendió a callar.

MEMOIRS OF A GEISHA
Arthur Golden

MEMORIAS DE UNA GEISHA
Arthur Golden
Translation Pilar Vázquez

Context
Published in 1997, Arthur Golden's debut novel *Memoirs of a Geisha* became an overnight success and was eventually turned into a film. Culling from his studies in Japanese history, Golden pens a first-person narrative of "fictional true confessions" from the point of view of a woman sold in childhood to become a geisha.

Translation
The excerpt of *Memoirs of a Geisha* included here is an interesting example of the use (or misuse) of a fictional translator's notes to give the impression that the text is a translation from another language; i.e. a pseudotranslation.

The translator's Spanish version of *Memoirs of a Geisha* exemplifies the creative liberty a translator has with texts: by changing the order of the phrases in the beginning lines to conform to Spanish expectations regarding cultural behaviors, the text maintains a similar level of discourse and credibility in both languages.

MEMOIRS OF A GEISHA
Arthur Golden

Translator's Note

One evening in the spring of 1936, when I was a boy of fourteen, my father took me to a dance performance in Kyoto. I remember only two things about it. The first is that he and I were the only Westerners in the audience; we had come from our home in the Netherlands only a few weeks earlier, so I had not yet adjusted to the cultural isolation and still felt it acutely. The second is how pleased I was, after months of intensive study of the Japanese language, to find that I could now understand fragments of the conversations I overheard. As for the young Japanese women dancing on the stage before me, I remember nothing of them except a vague impression of brightly colored kimono. I certainly had no way of knowing that in a time and place as far away as New York City nearly fifty years in the future, one among them would become my good friend and would dictate her extraordinary memoirs to me.

As a historian, I have always regarded memoirs as source material. A memoir provides a record not so much of the memoirist as of the memoirist's world. It must differ from biography in that a memoirist can never achieve the perspective that a biographer possesses as a matter of course. Autobiography, if there really is such a thing, is like asking a rabbit to tell us what he looks like hopping through the grasses of the field. How would he know? If we want to hear about the field, on the other hand, no one is in a better circumstance to tell us–so long as we keep in mind that we are missing all those things the rabbit was in no position to observe.

I say this with the certainty of an academician who has based a career on such distinctions. And yet I must confess that the memoirs of my dear friend Nitta Sayuri have impelled me to rethink my views. Yes, she does elucidate for us the very secret world in which she lived–the rabbit's view of the field, if you will. There may well be no better record of the strange life of a geisha than the one Sayuri offers.

MEMORIAS DE UNA GEISHA
Arthur Golden
Translation Pilar Vázquez

Nota del traductor

Cuando tenía catorce años, mi padre me llevó una noche, en Kioto, a un espectáculo de danza. Era la primavera de 1936. Sólo me acuerdo de dos cosas. La primera es que él y yo éramos los únicos occidentales del público; hacía tan sólo unas semanas que habíamos dejado nuestro hogar en Holanda y todavía no me había acostumbrado al aislamiento cultural, por eso lo recuerdo tan vívidamente. La segunda es lo contento que me sentí, tras meses de estudio intensivo del japonés, al darme cuenta de que entendía fragmentos de las conversaciones que oía a mi alrededor. De las jóvenes japonesas que bailaron ante mí en el estrado no recuerdo nada, salvo una vaga imagen de kimonos de brillantes colores. Por entonces no podía saber que casi cincuenta años después, en un lugar tan lejano como Nueva York, una de ellas se convertiría en una buena amiga mía y me dictaría sus memorias.

Como historiador que soy, siempre he considerado que las memorias constituyen un material de primera mano, que no sólo nos proporciona datos de la persona en cuestión, sino también del mundo en el que ha vivido. Difieren de la biografía en que el autor de las memorias nunca tiene el grado de perspectiva que, de por sí, suele poseer el biógrafo. La autobiografía, si es que tal cosa existe, es algo así como preguntarle a un conejo qué aspecto tiene cuando salta por el prado. ¿Cómo va a saberlo? Pero, por otro lado, si queremos saber algo del prado, nadie está en mejor posición que el conejo para decírnoslo, siempre que tengamos en cuenta que nos perderemos todas aquellas cosas que el conejo no haya observado debido a su posición en un momento dado.

Digo todo esto con la certeza del investigador cuya carrera está basada en esta suerte de distinciones. He de confesar, sin embargo, que las memorias de mi querida amiga Nitta Sayuri me obligaron a replantearme algunas de mis opiniones al respecto. Sí, ella nos muestra el mundo secreto en el que vivió; como si dijéramos, nos da la visión del prado desde el punto de vista del conejo. Posiblemente no haya una descripción mejor de la extraña vida de las geishas que la que aquí nos ofrece Sayuri.

THE STUDY OF LANGUAGE
George Yule

EL LENGUAJE
George Yule
Translation Nuria Bel Rafecas

Context
The Study of Language by George Yule is considered one of the most important introductions to the field of linguistics to date. In *The Study of Language* key elements of language such as its origins or the distinction between human, animal, sign or machine languages are analyzed while specific linguistic terms such as morphology, syntax or discourse analysis are explained.

Translation
The fact that *The Study of Language* is an academic text means, on one hand, that there is less room for interpretation than in a literary text, while, on the other, there is a need for a specialized vocabulary, in this case linguistic. The translator of this text must be able to match the linguistic and artistic creativity of the author and deal with specific equivalencies (e.g. onomatopoeic). This excerpt is an example of the need for a translator to intervene in a text to conform it to the reader.

THE STUDY OF LANGUAGE
George Yule

Arbitrariness

It is generally the case that there is no 'natural' connection between a linguistic form and its meaning. You cannot look at the Arabic word كلب, and from its shape, for example, determine that it has a natural meaning, any more than you can with its English translation form – *dog*. The linguistic form has no natural or 'iconic' relationship with that four-legged barking object out in the world. Recognizing this general fact about language leads us to conclude that a property of linguistic signs is their arbitrary relationship with the objects they are used to indicate. The forms of human language demonstrate a property called arbitrariness – they do not, in any way, 'fit' the objects they denote. Of course, you can play a game with words to make them 'fit', in some sense, the property or activity they indicate, as in these examples from a child's game:

However, such a game only emphasizes how arbitrary the connection normally is between the linguistic form and its meaning.

There are, of course, some words in language which have sounds which seem to 'echo' the sounds of objects or activities. English examples might be *cuckoo*, *crash* or *slurp*, which are onomatopoeic, and which we have already noted (Chapter 1) as part of the 'natural sounds' theory of language origin. In most languages, these onomatopoeic words are relatively rare, and the vast majority of linguistic expressions are in fact arbitrary.

EL LENGUAJE
George Yule
Translation Nuria Bel Rafecas

Arbitrariedad

Lo normal es que no haya una conexión natural entre una forma lingüística y su significado. Mirando la palabra árabe ـﻠﻛ, por ejemplo, no podemos determinar que tiene un significado natural a partir únicamente de su forma gráfica, o no más de lo que lo podemos hacer de su traducción castellana *perro*. La forma lingüística no tiene una relación natural o icónica con ese objeto ladrador de cuatro patas que hay en el mundo. El reconocer este hecho general del lenguaje nos lleva a decir que una propiedad de los signos lingüísticos es su relación arbitraria con los objetos que indican. Las formas del lenguaje humano demuestran una propiedad llamada *arbitrariedad*: no pueden, de ninguna forma, adecuarse a los objetos que denotan. Claro que, si queremos, podemos jugar a hacer que las palabras correspondan de alguna forma a la propiedad o actividad que indican, como en estos ejemplos de un juego infantil:

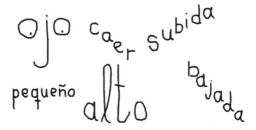

Sin embargo, un juego así sólo pone énfasis en lo arbitrario de la conexión que normalmente hay entre la forma lingüística y su significado.

Es evidente que hay algunas palabras en las diferentes lenguas que suenan como imitaciones de los sonidos de algunos objetos o actividades. Algunos ejemplos del castellano son *cucú, arrullar, tartamudear* o *ronronear*, que son onomatopéyicos y que ya hemos mencionado al hablar de la teoría del origen del lenguaje de los sonidos naturales (en el Capítulo 1). Sin embargo, en la mayoría de las lenguas estas palabras son relativamente escasas y la mayor parte de las expresiones son, de hecho, arbitrarias.

TITLE VI OF THE CIVIL RIGHTS ACT OF 1964
U.S. Department of Health and Human Services

TÍTULO VI DEL ACTA DE
LOS DERECHOS CIVILES DE 1964
Departamento de Salud y Servicios Humanos de los EE.UU.

Context

This text is a Fact Sheet published by the Office for Civil Rights of the U.S Department of Health and Human Services. "Your Rights under Title VI of the Civil Rights Act of 1964" interprets Title VI in lay terms and can be found on line in English, Spanish, Chinese, Korean, Polish, Russian and Tagalog. The translations supplied for Vietnamese do not pertain as much to Civil Rights issues and do not include this specific one.

Translation

As occurs with translations of government agencies or large corporations, this Fact Sheet does not give credit to the translator or the writer. Due to the quasi-legal nature of the text, the translation is quite literal; i.e. the Spanish follows the English word order as closely as possible. Not only is the English easily 'recognizable' in the translation, but the integrity of the Spanish language is at times compromised. For example, conventional norms such as capitalizations are disregarded, verb forms are foreignized and false friends are allowed.

The presentation of the two Fact Sheets are almost identical, although the Spanish version 'speaks' more visually (with checks and crosses instead of the bullet points of the English). Other differences between the two versions are the clarifications of government agencies and acronyms and the use of English technological words in the Spanish translation.

TITLE VI OF THE CIVIL RIGHTS ACT OF 1964
U.S. Department of Health and Human Services

What Is Title VI?
Title VI of the Civil Rights Act of 1964 is a national law that protects persons from discrimination based on their race, color, or national origin in programs and activities that receive Federal financial assistance. If you are eligible for Medicaid, other health care, or human services, you cannot be denied assistance because of your race, color, or national origin. The Office for Civil Rights (OCR) in the U. S. Department of Health and Human Services (DHHS) enforces Title VI as well as other civil rights laws.

Some of the institutions or programs that may be covered by Title VI are:
- Extended care facilities
- Public assistance programs
- Nursing homes
- Adoption agencies
- Hospitals
- Day care centers
- Mental health centers
- Senior citizen centers
- Medicaid and Medicare
- Family health centers and clinics
- Alcohol and drug treatment centers

Prohibited Discriminatory Acts
There are many forms of illegal discrimination based on race, color, or national origin that frequently limit the opportunities of minorities to gain equal access to services. A recipient of Federal financial assistance may not, based on race, color, or national origin:
- Deny services, financial aid or other benefits provided as a part of health or human service programs.
- Provide a different service, financial aid or other benefit, or provide them in a different manner from those provided to others under the program.
- Segregate or separately treat individuals in any matter related to the receipt of any service, financial aid or other benefit....

More common discriminatory practices are identified in the DHHS Title VI regulation found at 45 CFR Part 80.

For information on how to file a complaint of discrimination, or to obtain information of a civil rights nature, please contact us. OCR employees will make every effort to provide prompt service.

TÍTULO VI DEL ACTA DE
LOS DERECHOS CIVILES DE 1964
Departamento de Salud y Servicios Humanos de los EE.UU.
Translator unknown

¿Que Es El Título VI?

El Título VI del Acta de Derechos Civiles de 1964, es una ley nacional que protege a las personas de la discriminación basada en su raza, color, u origen nacional, en programas o actividades que reciben asistencia financiera Federal. Si usted es elegible para recibir Medicaid, algún otro plan de cuidado médico, o servicios humanos, a usted no se le pueden negar esos servicios por razones de su raza, color u origen nacional. La Oficina para los Derechos Civiles ("Office for Civil Rights" u "OCR") en el Departamento de Salud y Servicios Humanos de los Estados Unidos (o "DHHS") hace cumplir el Título VI como también otras leyes de derechos civiles.

Algunas de las instituciones o programas que pueden ser cubiertos por el Título VI son:
√ Facilidades de cuidados extendidos.
√ Programas de Asistencia Pública.
√ Casas para ancianos.
√ Agencias de adopción
√ Hospitales.
√ Centros de cuidados infantiles o guarderías.
√ Centros de cuidado psiquiátrico.
√ Centros de personas mayores.
√ Medicaid y Medicare.
√ Centros y clínicas de salud familiar
√ Centros de tratamiento de alcoholismo y drogadicción.

Actos Discriminatorios Prohibidos:

Hay muchas formas de discriminación ilegal basada en la raza, color u origen nacional, que frecuentemente limitan las oportunidades de las minorías a tener igual acceso a los servicios. Una entidad que reciba ayuda Federal no puede, basada en la raza, el color o el origen nacional:
x Negar servicios, ayuda financiera, u otros beneficios provistos como parte de los programas de salud y servicios humanos.
x Proveer un servicio, ayuda financiera u otro beneficio en forma diferente, o proveerlos en una manera diferente de aquella provista a otros, bajo el mismo programa.
x Segregar o tratar separadamente a algunos individuos en cualquier materia relacionada con la recepción de cualquier servicio, ayuda financiera u otro beneficio...

PEANUTS
Charles Schulz

PEANUTS
Charles Schulz
Translator unknown

Context
"Peanuts" is a comic strip known the world over. Translated into more than 40 languages and appearing in more than 2,500 newspapers in 75 countries, Charles Schulz published his famous characters from 1950 to 2000.

Translation
This comic strip is not difficult except for the onomatopoeia of the second frame –an element which too often remains untranslated due to the difficulty of changing the graphics of texts (e.g. the interrogative signs and exclamatory signs of the third frame). This strip (specifically the fourth frame) has been localized to a specific regional Spanish.

PEANUTS
Charles Schulz

PEANUTS
Charles Schulz
Translator unknown

COULD YOU BE AT RISK FOR DIABETES?
American Diabetes Association

¿PODRÍA USTED ESTAR A RIESGO DE TENER DIABETES?
American Diabetes Association

Context
This excerpt belongs to an informational brochure on Diabetes put out by the American Diabetes Association, one side in English and the other in Spanish. While both texts are laid out and presented in an identical fashion, there are two sections on the Spanish side that are longer. This an excellent example of an translation expanded by an organization as they look to target a specific audience, in this case justified by the fact that the Latino population in the U.S. has double the cases of diabetes than non-Latinos.

Translation
The Spanish translations of the sections included here are much longer than the original English (342 Spanish words vs. 267 in English). Although the two sides of the brochure are visually identical, two of the Spanish sections are in fact expanded versions rather than translations; "¿Qué es la diabetes" and "¿Sabía qué?" contain a greater amount of information than their corresponding English sections.

At the discourse level, it is interesting to note that the assertiveness of the English is culturally targeted and therefore 'tamed' for the Hispanic group (e.g. **NOW** vs. *hoy mismo*). It is unfortunate that translations such as these are not held as accountable as their source texts –perhaps if there were a better system of checks and balances in the process of translation, target texts would be more respected. Neither the source text nor the target text identify the writer.

COULD YOU BE AT RISK FOR DIABETES?
American Diabetes Association

Are You at Risk? Take this Test.
Know Your Score.
Find out if you are at risk for having diabetes **NOW**. Write in the points next to each statement that is true for you. If a statement is not **true**, put a zero. Then add your total score.

• I am a woman who has had a baby weighing more than nine pounds at birth............................	Yes	1	_____
• I have a sister or brother with diabetes.................	Yes	1	_____
• I have a parent with diabetes..............................	Yes	1	_____
• My weight is equal to or above that listed in the chart..	Yes	5	_____
• I am under 65 years of age <u>and</u> I get little or no exercise..	Yes	5	_____
• I am between 45 and 64 years of age..................	Yes	5	_____
• I am 65 years old or older....................................	Yes	9	_____
		TOTAL	_____

If You Scored 10 or More Points
Your are at high risk for having diabetes. Only your health care provider can check to see if you have diabetes. See yours soon and find out for sure.

What is Diabetes?
Diabetes means that your blood sugar is too high. Your blood always has some sugar in it because the body needs sugar for energy to keep you going. But too much sugar in the blood is not good for your health.

What Can You Do?
You can do things now to lower your risk for diabetes by:
• Keeping your weight in control
• Staying active most days of the week
• Eating low fat meals that are high in fruits, vegetables, and whole grain foods.

¿PODRÍA USTED ESTAR A RIESGO DE TENER DIABETES?
American Diabetes Association
Translator unknown

¿Está Usted a Riesgo De Tener Diabetes?

Conozca si usted está a riesgo de tener diabetes hoy mismo. Escriba los resultados a la par de cada oración que sea **cierta** para usted. Si una oración no es cierta para usted, ponga un cero. Después sume el total de los resultados.

1.	Yo soy una mujer que tuvo un bebé que pesó más de 9 libras al nacer	Sí	1	___
2.	Yo tengo una hermana o un hermano con diabetes	Sí	1	___
3.	Uno de mis padres tiene diabetes	Sí	1	___
4.	Mi peso es igual o está por encima del indicado en la tabla	Sí	5	___
5.	Tengo menos de 65 años de edad y hago poco o nada de ejercicio	Sí	5	___
6.	Yo tengo entre 45 y 64 años de edad	Sí	5	___
7.	Yo tengo 65 años de edad o más	Sí	9	___
			TOTAL	___

Si su resultado es de 10 o más puntos

Usted tiene un alto riesgo de tener diabetes. Sólo un doctor puede determinar si usted tiene diabetes. Visite a un doctor pronto y averigüe para poder estar seguro.

¿Qué es la Diabetes?

La diabetes es una enfermedad que afecta la forma en que su cuerpo usa la comida. Su cuerpo cambia los alimentos que usted come en azúcar de la sangre. Las células del cuerpo usan el azúcar en la sangre como energía.

Algunas personas no pueden llevar el azúcar de la sangre a las células. El azúcar se acumula en la sangre.

Con el tiempo, esta acumulación de azúcar es la causante de la ceguera, un ataque al corazón, perder un pie o la pierna en una amputación, de que los riñones paren de trabajar o puede hasta matarlo.

¿Sabía Usted?

• Que comer azúcar no causa diabetes.
• Que usted puede sentirse bien y todavía tener diabetes.
• Que no hay cura para la diabetes, **pero usted puede controlarla.**

DRACULA
Tod Browning

DRÁCULA
George Melford
Translation/adaptation Baltasar Fernández Cue

Context
The film "Dracula" (Universal Studios, 1931) is based on Bram Stoker's novel, although it leans heavily on the theater adaptation by Hamilton Deane and John L. Balderston.

Translation
As happened often at the time, this movie was filmed twice: once in English and then in Spanish. For 22 nights, after *Dracula* was finished filming for the day, a Spanish-speaking cast would take over the set to film the same film in Spanish. Although the two versions are based on almost identical scripts, the Spanish version by Baltasar Fernández Cue is longer (104 minutes to the 78 in English) in part because Carlos Villarías (or Villar), who played Count Dracula, spoke much more slowly than Bela Lugosi. and in part, because of the minor differences in the directors' work– Tod Browning's Spanish-version counterpart was George Melfrod. (Melford, who didn't speak Spanish, was aided by Enrique Tova Avalos.)

Not only is the Spanish version longer, but also less subdued –Lupita Tovar's dresses were tighter and showed more cleavage than Helen Chandler's. The Spanish-speaking audience was also permitted to see the vampire bite marks, eliminated in Hollywood alongside the biting of men to avoid possible homosexual inferences. Noteworthy in this excerpt are the cultural differences such as the expanded niceties exchanged between Renfield and the Innkeeper's wife in Spanish.

The versions of *Dracula* presented here are the opening scenes of first, the English-speaking film version; second, the Spanish subtitles of the English version; and third, the Spanish version, filmed in 1931 (personal transcription). Not included are the English subtitles of the Spanish version, in fact, a back-translation.

DRACULA
Tod Browning

YOUNG WOMAN: "Among the rugged peaks that frown down upon the Borgo Pass are found crumbling castles of a bygone age."

RENFIELD: I say, driver, a bit slower.

COACHMAN: Oh, no! Must reach the inn before sundown!

MADAM: And why, pray?

MAN: It is Walpurgis Night, the night of evil! Nosferatu!

MAN: On this night, madam, the doors, they are barred and to the Virgin we pray.

RENFIELD: I say, porter, don't take my luggage down. I'm going on to Borgo Pass tonight.

RENFIELD: No, no, please, put that back up there.

INNKEEPER: The driver, he is afraid. Walpurgis night. Good fellow, he is. He wants me to ask if you can wait and go on after sunrise.

RENFIELD: Well, I'm sorry, but there's a carriage meeting me at Borgo Pass at midnight.

INNKEEPER: Borgo Pass?

RENFIELD: Yes.

INNKEEPER: Whose carriage?

RENFIELD: Count Dracula's.

INNKEEPER: Count Dracula's?

RENFIELD: Yes.

INNKEEPER: Castle Dracula?

RENFIELD: Yes, that's where I'm going.

INNKEEPER: To the castle?

RENFIELD: Yes.

INNKEEPER: No, you mustn't go there. We people of the mountains believe at the castle there are vampires! Dracula and his wives! They take the form of wolves and bats. They leave their coffins at night, and they feed on the blood of the living.

RENFIELD: Oh, but that's all superstition. Why I... I can't understand why...

INNKEEPER: Look, the sun! When it is gone, they leave their coffins. Come, we must go indoors.

RENFIELD: But, wait. I mean, just a minute, I.... What I'm trying to say is that I'm not afraid. I've explained to the driver that it's a matter of business with me. I've got to go, really. Well, good night.

INNKEEPER'S WIFE: Wait! Please, If you must go, wear this for your mother's sake. It will protect you.

DRÁCULA
Tod Browning
Translator unknown

JOVEN: "Entre las cumbres abruptas que enmarcan el Desfiladero de Borgo se encuentran ruinosos castillos de una época remota–"."

RENFIELD: Cochero, un poco más lento.

COCHERO: Ah, no. Hay que llegar a la posada antes de que caiga la noche.

SEÑORA: ¿Y por qué, dígame?

VIAJERO: Hoy es la noche de Walpurgis. La noche del mal. Nosferatu–

VIAJERO: En esta noche señora todas las puertas están atrancadas y le rezamos a la virgen.

RENFIELD: Oiga, mozo, no baje mi equipaje. Esta noche partiré al Desfiladero de Borgo.

RENFIELD: No, no, por favor, póngalo de vuelta.

POSADERO: El cochero tiene miedo. Es la noche de Walpurgis. Es un buen hombre. Desea saber si Ud. puede continuar el viaje después del amanecer.

RENFIELD: Lo siento, me espera un coche en el Desfiladero de Borgo a medianoche.

POSADERO: ¿En el Desfiladero de Borgo?

RENFIELD: Sí.

POSADERO: ¿El coche de quién?

RENFIELD: Del Conde Drácula.

POSADERO: [no subtitle]

RENFIELD: Sí.

POSADERO: ¿El castillo Drácula??

RENFIELD: Sí, ahí es donde voy.

POSADERO: ¿Al castillo?

RENFIELD: Sí.

POSADERO: No debe de ir allí. La gente de las montañas creemos que en el castillo hay vampiros. Drácula y sus esposas. Se transforman en lobos y murciélagos. Por la noche dejan sus ataúdes y se alimentan de la sangre de los vivos.

RENFIELD: Pero eso es sólo una superstición. No comprendo por qué–

POSADERO: Mire. El sol. Cuando desaparece, dejan sus ataúdes. Venga. Debemos ir adentro.

RENFIELD: Espere– Un minuto. Lo que trato de decirle es que no tengo miedo. Le expliqué al cochero que se trata de negocios. Debo ir allí. De veras. Bueno, buenas noches.

POSADERA: Espere. Por favor. Si debe ir, póngase esto. Por amor a su madre. Lo protegerá.

DRÁCULA
George Melford
Translation/adaptation Baltasar Fernández Cue

COCHERO: ¡Arre!

SARA: "Cerca de Bistritz la carretera tuerce hacia el corazón de los Cárpatos, uno de los lugares más agrestes y menos conocidos de Europa."

RENFIELD: A ver, permítame.

SARA: Muchas gracias.

VIAJERA: ¿Dónde íbamos Sara?

COCHERO: ¡Arre! ¡Arre!

SARA: "...uno de los lugares más agrestes y menos conocidos de Europa."

VIAJERA: Siga.

SARA: "Entre sus cumbres abruptas se encuentran ruinosos castillos, restos de una época remota."

REINFELD: ¡Cochero, a ver si va un poco más despacio!

VIAJERO: No, no, hay que llegar a la posada antes de la noche.

SARA: ¿Y por qué?

VIAJERO: Hoy es *Walpurgis Nacht*, noche de mal agüero. ¡Nosferatu! Los muertos salen de las tumbas y chupan la sangre de los vivos.

VIAJERA: Ah, mira que ridículo este.

VIAJERO: Ud. no burlar si vivir aquí. Esta noche todas las puertas atrancadas. Y nosotros rezar a la Virgen.

VOCES: Buen viaje...Muchas gracias....Vaya, me alegro...

RENFIELD: Mozo no baje mi equipaje. Yo tengo que seguir hasta el desfiladero de Borgo.

SEÑORA: Muy buen viaje hemos tenido. Y ustedes ¿cómo han estado?

POSADERO: Debo advertirle que hoy es el día de Santa Walpurgas, que es de mal agüero por aquí y el cochero, je, je, es un buen hombre... desea saber si le es a usted lo mismo continuar el viaje después del amanecer.

RENFIELD: Lo siento mucho pero a las doce me esperará un coche en el desfiladero de Borgo.

POSADERO: ¿Qué coche?

RENFIELD: El del Conde Drácula.

POSADERO: ¡El castillo de Drácula!

RENFIELD: Eso es, allí es adonde voy.

SEÑORA: Fíjese, quiere irse esta noche al desfiladero de Borgo.

POSADERO: Yo le suplico permanezca aquí esta noche.

RENFIELD: Pero si todo eso no pasa de ser superstición. Quiero decir, que en una región montañosa como ésta, no comprendo cómo... Después de todo, lo que yo trato de decir es que yo no tengo miedo. Ya le he dicho que se trata de negocios. Tengo que ir allí. De veras.

SEÑORA: Espere. Ya que quiere irse, póngase esto. Póngaselo, por lo que más quiera. Le servirá de protección.

RENFIELD: Gracias.

SEÑORA: No se merecen.

RENFIELD: Buenas noches.

SEÑORA: Buenas noches y le deseo buen viaje.

PÚBLICO: Buenas noches. Buenas noches. Que lo pase bien. Buenas noches. Adiós.

SARA: ¿Oiga, cree usted que de veras hay vampiros que salen de las tumbas al anochecer y andan por allí en busca de sangre?

POSADERO: Yo he visto las víctimas.

SARA: ¡Ay!

SEÑORA: Vamos Sara.

Bibliography

Agosín, Marjorie. 1986. *Brujas y algo más / Witches and Other Things.* Trans. Cola Franzen. Pittsburgh, Pennsylvania: Latin American Literary Press.

Allison, Young. 1924. *The Infinite Passion Being the Celebrated Rimas and the Letters to an Unknown Woman of Gustavo Adolfo Becquer,* Chicago: Walter M. Hill.

Altabe, David. 1974. *Symphony of Love. Las Rimas.* Trans. David Altabe, Long Beach, New York: Regina Publishing House.

American Diabetes Association. 2006. "Could You Be at Risk for Diabetes?" / "¿Podría usted estar a riesgo de tener diabetes?" Alexandria, VA: American Diabetes Association.

Anderman, Gunilla and Margaret Rogers, eds. 1999. *Word, Text, Translation, Liber Amicorum for Peter Newmark.* Clevedon: Multilingual Matters.

Arnold, Doud J., Lorna Balkan, Siety Meijer, R. Lee Humphreys and Louisa Sadler. 1994. *Machine Translation: An Introductory Guide.* Cambridge, MA and Oxford: Blackwell.

Ashcroft, Bill, Gareth Griffiths and Helen Tiffin. 1989. *The Empire Writes Back: Theory and Practice in Postcolonial Literatures.* London and New York: Routledge.

Baker, Mona. 1992. *In Other Words: A Coursebook on Translation.* London and New York: Routledge.

——. 1993. "Corpus Linguistics and Translation Studies. Implications and Applications." In *Text and Technology: In Honour of John Sinclair,* Mona Baker, Gill Frances and Elena Tognini-Bonelli, eds. Amsterdam: John Benjamins, 233-250.

——. ed. 2004. *Routledge Encyclopedia of Translation Studies.* London and New York: Routledge.

Bassnett, Susan. 2002. *Translation Studies.* London and New York: Routledge.

Bassnett, Susan and Harish Trivedi, eds. 1999. *Post-colonial Translation. Theory and Practice.* London and New York: Routledge.

Bécquer, Gustavo Adolfo. 1973. *Obras completas.* Madrid: Aguilar.

Beeby Lonsdale, Allison. 1996. *Teaching Translation from Spanish to English. Worlds Beyond Words.* Ottawa: University of Ottawa Press.

Bell, Roger T. 1991. *Translation and Translating.* New York: Longman.

Benjamin, Walter. 1969. "The Task of the Translator." Trans. James Hynd and M. Valk, *Delos* 2: 90.

Berman, Antoine. 2003. "Translation and the Trials of the Foreign." In Lawrence Venuti, ed. 284-297.

Biguenet, John and Rainer Schulte, eds. 1989. *The Craft of Translation.* Chicago: The University of Chicago Press.

Blum-Kulka, Shoshana. 1986. "Shifts of Cohesion and Coherence in Translation." In *Interlingual and Intercultural Communication. Discourse and Cognition in Translation and Second Language Acquisition,* Juliane House and Shoshana Blum-Kulka, eds. Tübingen: Gunter Narr, 17-35.

Bosch Benítez, Amalia. 2002. "La traducción o adaptación de textos rimados en cuentos tradicionales y literarios en Ursula K. Le Guin *El viaje de Salomón.*" In *Traducción y literatura infantil,* Isabel Febles, Elisa Ramón Molina, Ángeles Perera Santana, Gisela Marcelo Wirnitzer, eds. Universidad de Las Palmas de Gran Canaria: Ediciones ULPGC, 133-143.

Cabrera Infante, Guillermo. 1998. *Tres tristes tigres.* Barcelona: Seix Barral.

——. *Three Trapped Tigers.* 1971. Trans. Donald Gardner, Suzanne Jill Levine in collaboration with the author. New York: Harper & Row.

Castro Paniagua, Francisco. 2000. *English-Spanish Translation, through a Cross-Cultural Interpretation Approach.* Lanham: University Press of America.

Catford, John C. 1965. *A Linguistic Theory of Translation.* London: Oxford University Press.

Cheyfitz, Eric. 1991. *The Poetics of Imperialism: Translation and Colonization from the Tempest to Tarzan.* New York and Oxford: Oxford University Press.

Child, Jack. 1992. *Introduction to Spanish Translation.* Lanham: University Press of America.

Cicero, Marco Tulius. 1976. "De optimo genere oratorum." In *De Inventione, De Optimo Genere, Oratorum, Topica.* Trans. H. M. Hubbell. Cambridge: Harvard UP. 1-348.

Cisneros, Sandra. 2003. *Caramelo.* Trans. Liliana Valenzuela. Waterville, ME: Throndike Press.

Coetzee, J. M. 1983. *Life & Times of Michael K,* London: Penguin Books.

——. 1987. *Vida y época de Michael K.* 1987. Trans. Concha Manella. Madrid: Ediciones Alfaguara.

——. 2006. *Vida y época de Michael K.* Revised trans. Concha Manella. Barcelona: Mondadori.

Croft-Cooke, Rupert. 1927. *Twenty Poems from the Spanish of Bécquer, With an Introductory Note on his Life and Work,* Oxford: Basil Blackwell.

Cronin, Michael. 1996. *Translating Ireland.* Cork: Cork University Press.

Diaz del Castillo, Bernal. 1942. *Historia verdadera de la conquista de la Nueva España.* Madrid: Espasa Calpe.

Dolet, Étienne. 1997. "How to Translate Well from One Language into Another." Trans. D. G. Ross. In *Western Translation Theory from Herodotus to Nietzsche,* Douglas Robinson, ed. Manchester: St. Jerome.

Dracula. 1931. Tod Browning and George Melford, directors. Universal Pictures.

Dryden, John. 1961. "Preface to *Ovid's Epistles.*" In *Essays of John Dryden*, William P. Ker, ed. New York: Russell.

Duff, Alan. 1981. *The Third Language*. New York: Pergamon Press.

Eades, Diana. 2003a. "The Participation of Second Language and Second Dialect Speakers in the Legal System." *Annual Review of Applied Linguistics* 23: 113-133.

Fawcett, Peter. 2004. "Linguistic Approaches." In Mona Baker, ed., 120-125.

Fédération Internationale des Traducteurs (FIT). 1994. "The Translator's Charter." UNESCO.

Gamal, Muhhamad. 2004. "Court Interpreting." In Mona Baker, ed., 53-56.

García Yebra, Valentín. 1984. *Teoría y práctica de la traducción*. Madrid: Editorial Gredos, S.A.

Golden, Arthur. 1997. *Memoirs of a geisha*. New York: Random House.

———. 2002. *Memorias de una Geisha*. Trans. Pilar Vázquez. Madrid: Santillana Ediciones Generales.

Gouadec, Daniel. 1989. "Traduction Signalétique." In *Meta* 35 (2), 332-41.

Gregory, Michael. 1980. "Perspectives on Translation from the Firthian Tradition." *Meta* 25 (4): 455-66.

Gresset, Michel and Patrick Samway. 1983. *Faulkner and Idealism: Perspectives from Paris*. University Press of Mississippi.

Halliday, M.A.K. 1978. *Language as Social Semiotic*. New York: Arnold.

Harris, Brian. 1988. "Bi-Text, a New Concept in Translation Theory." In *Language Monthly* Num. 54, 8-10.

Hatim, Basil and Ian Mason. 1990. *Discourse and the Translator*. New York: Longman.

Hermans, Theo. 1985. *The Manipulation of Literature*. London: Croon Helm.

Herodotus. 1914. *Histories*. Trans. George Campbell Macaulay. Project Gutenberg.

Hervey, Sándor, Ian Higgins and Louise M. Haywood. 1995. *Thinking Spanish Translation. A Course in Translation Method: Spanish to English*. London and New York: Routledge.

Hill, Sam and William Bradford. 2000. *Bilingual Grammar of English-Spanish Syntax*. Lanham: University Press of America.

Holmes, James. 2003. "The Name and Nature of Translation Studies." In Lawrence Venuti, ed., 172-185.

Horace, Quintus Horatius Flaccus. 1971."Ars Poetica" / "The Art of Poetry." Trans E. C. Wickham. In *Critical Theory Since Plato*, Hazard Adams, ed. New York: Harcourt Brace Jovanovich, 68- 75.

House, Juliane. 1977. *A Model for Translation Quality Assessment*, Tübingen: Gunter Narr.

———. 1997. *A Model for Translation Quality Assessment: A Model Revisited*. Tübingen: Gunter Narr.

Innsly, Owen. 1902. *Love Songs and Other Poems*, New York: Grafton Press.

Jackobson, Roman. 1992. "On Linguistic Aspects of Translation." In Rainer Schulte and John Biguenet, eds., 144-151.

Jiménez Barca, Antonio. 2006. "El negocio de inventar nombres." Madrid: Spain, *El País*, 6/18/06.
——. 2006. "Hallowed be thy name." Madrid, Spain: *El País, English Edition*, 6/20/06.
Kelly, Louis G. 1979. *The True Interpreter: A History of Translation Theory and Practice in the West.* New York: Saint Martin's Press.
Klaudy, Kinga and Krisztina Károly. 2005. "Implicitation in Translation: Empirical evidence for operational asymmetry in translation." In *Across Languages and Cultures*, Vol. 6, Num. 1, April, 13-28.
Koller, Werner. 1989. "Equivalence in Translation Theory." Trans. Andrew Chesterman. In *Readings in Translation Theory*, Andrew Chesterman, ed. Helsinki: Oy Finn Lectura Ab., 99-104.
Larson, Mildred L. 1998. *Meaning-Based Translation. A Guide to Cross-Language Equivalence.* Lanham: University Press of America.
Lefevere, André. 1992. *Translation, Rewriting, and the Manipulation of Literary Fame.* London and New York: Routledge.
Levine, Suzanne Jill. 1991. *The Subversive Scribe. Translating Latin American Fiction.* Saint Paul: Graywolf Press.
Lewis, Philip E. 1985. "The Measure of Translation Effects." In *Difference in Translation*, Joseph F. Graham, ed. Ithaca: Cornell University Press.
López, Guix, Juan Gabriel and Jacqueline Minett Wilkinson. 2003. *Manual de traducción inglés / castellano. Teoría y práctica.* Barcelona: Gedisa.
López Morales, Humberto. 1982. "Estructuras internas, estructuras externas y traducción." In *Problemas de la Traducción / Problems in Translation.* Puerto Rico: Editorial de la Universidad de Puerto Rico.
——. 1982. "Deep Structures, Surface Structures and Translation." Trans. María Esther Castro. In *Problemas de la Traducción / Problems in Translation.* Puerto Rico: Editorial de la Universidad de Puerto Rico.
Lunn, Patricia V. and Ernest Lunsford. 2003. *En otras palabras. Perfeccionamiento del español por medio de la traducción.* Washington D.C.: Georgetown University Press.
Malinowski, Bronislaw. 1932. "The Problem of Meaning in Primitive Languages." In *The Meaning of Meaning*, C. K. Ogden and I. A. Richards, eds. London: Kegan Paul.
Manella, Concepción. 2000. "A Brotherhood of Voices: William Faulkner's *Absalom, Absalom!*" In *William Faulkner in Venice*, Rosella Mamoli and Pia Masiero, eds. Venezia: Marsilio Editori.
Martí, José. 1997. *Versos sencillos / Simple verses.* Trans. Manuel A. Tellechea. Houston, TX: Arte Público Press.
——. 2005. *Versos sencillos. A Dual Language Edition.* Trans. Anne Fountain. Jefferson, North Carolina and London: McFarland & Company, Inc.
Miller, Elizabeth. 2005. "Applying Theory to the Practice of Literary Translation: Contemporary Latin American Authors." In *Translation Review*, Num. 69. University of Texas at Dallas, 43-48.
Munday, Jeremy. 2001. *Introducing Translation Studies. Theories and Applications.* London and New York: Routledge, 2001.

Newmark, Peter. 1982. *Approaches to Translation.* Oxford: Pergamon Institute of English.

———. 1988. *A Textbook of Translation.* New York: Prentice Hall.

———. 1991. *About Translation.* Multilingual Matters, Ltd.

Nida, Eugene. 1964. *Toward a Science of Translation.* Leiden: E. J. Brill.

Nida, Eugene A. and Charles R. Taber. 1969. *The Theory and Practice of Translation.* Leiden: E.I. Brill.

Niranjana, Tejaswini. 1992. *Siting Translation. History, Post-structuralism, and the Colonial Context.* Berkeley: University of California Press.

Nolan, James. 2005. *Interpretation. Techniques and Exercises.* Clevedon: Multilingual Matters, Ltd.

Nord, Christiane. 1991a. *Text Analysis in Translation.* Amsterdam and Atlanta, Rodopi.

Paz, Octavio. 1971. *Traducción: literatura y literalidad.* Barcelona: Tusquets.

———. 1986. "On Translation." UNESCO Courier, May-June.

Pérez Reverte, Arturo. 1988. *El maestro de esgrima.* Barcelona: Mondadori.

———. 1998. *The Fencing Master.* Trans. Margaret Jull Costa. San Diego: Harcourt Books.

Pinker, Steven. 1994. *The Language Instinct.* New York: William Morrow.

Popovic, Anton. 1970. "The Concept 'Shift of Expression' in Translation Analysis." In *The Nature of Translation. Essays of the Theory and Practice of Literary Translation,* James Holmes, Frans de Haan and Anton Popovic, eds. The Hague: Mouton.

Pym, Anthony and Horst Turk. 2004. "Translatability." In Mona Baker, ed., 273-277.

Rabassa, Gregory. 1989. "No Two Snowflakes Are Alike." In John Biguenet and Rainer Schulte, eds., 1-12.

———. 2005. *If This Be Treason. Translation and Its Dyscontents. A Memoir.* New York: New Directions.

Reiss, Katharina. 1989. "Text Types, Translation Types and Translation Assessment." In *Readings in Translation Theory,* Andrew Chesterman ed. Helsinki: Oy Finn Lectura Ab., 105-115.

———. 2003. "Type, Kind and Individuality of Text: Decision Making in Translation." Trans. Susan Kitron. In Lawrence Venuti, ed., 160-171.

Reiss, Katharina and Hans Vermeer. 1984. *Grundlegung einer allgemeinen Translationstheorie,* Tübingen: Niemeyer.

Renard, Jules. 1908. *Rimas of Gustavo Becquer,* Boston: Richard C. Badger, Gorham Press.

Risset, Jacqueline. 1984. "Joyce Translates Joyce." In *Comparative Criticism, Translation in Theory and Practice,* Vol 6. Cambridge University Press.

Rivera, Tomás. 1983. *...y no se lo tragó la tierra / ...and the Earth Did Not Part.* Trans. Herminio Ríos. Berkeley, California: Editorial Justa Publications.

———. 1995. *...And the Earth Did Not Devour Him.* Trans. Evangelina Vigil-Piñon. Houston, Texas: Arte Público Press.

Robinson, Douglas, ed. 1997b. *Western Translation Theory from Herodotus to Nietzsche.* Manchester: St. Jerome.

———. 2000. *Becoming a Translator.* London and New York: Routledge.

——. 2004. "Paraphrase." In Mona Baker, ed., 166-167.

Samuelsson-Brown, Geoffrey. 1998. *A Practical Guide for Translators*. Clevendon: Multilingual Matters, Ltd.

Santoyo, Julio César. 1996. *El delito de traducir*. León: Universidad de León.

Sayers Peden, Margaret. 1989. "Building a Translation, the Reconstruction Business: Poem 145 of Sor Juana Inés de la Cruz." In John Biguenet and Rainer Schulte, eds., 13-27.

Schleiermacher, Friedrich. 1977. "On the Different Methods of Translating." Trans. André Lefevere. In *Translating Literature*, 67-89.

Schulte, Hans and Gerhart Teuscher, eds. 1993. *The Art of Literary Translation*. Lanham: University Press of America.

Schulte, Rainer and John Biguenet, eds. 1992. *Theories of Translation. An Anthology of Essays from Dryden to Derrida*. Chicago: The University of Chicago Press.

Seco, Manuel. 2003. *Gramática esencial del español*. Madrid: Espasa Calpe.

Schulz, Charles. 1990. "Peanuts." United Media. 6/18/90.

Shuttleworth, Mark and Moira Cowie. 1997. *Dictionary of Translation Studies*. Manchester, UK: St Jerome Publishing.

Simon, Sherry. 1996. *Gender in Translation. Cultural Identity and the Politics of Transmission*. London and New York: Routledge.

Snell-Hornby, Mary. 1995. *Translation Studies: An Integrated Approach*, Amsterdam and Philadelphia: John Benjamins.

Sommer, Doris, ed. 2003. *Bilingual Games. Some Literary Investigations*. New York: Palgrave Macmillan.

Spivak, Gayatri. 2003. *Outside in the Teaching Machine*. London and New York: Routledge.

Stavans, Ilan. 1995. *The Hispanic Condition*. New York: Harper Collins Publisher.

Steiner, George. 1975. *After Babel*. New York: Oxford University Press.

Sullivan, Henry W. 2002. *The Poems of Gustavo Adolfo Bécquer: A Metrical, Linear Translation*. Rock Hill, South Carolina: Spanish Literature Publications Company.

Toury, Gideon. 1995. *Descriptive Translation Studies and Beyond*. Amsterdam: John Benjamins.

Tymoczko, Maria and Edwin Gentzler. 2002. *Translation and Power*. Amherst and Boston: University of Massachusetts Press.

Tytler, Alexander. 1978. *Essay on the Principles of Translation*. Amsterdam: John Benjamins.

Valero-Garcés, Carmen. 1995. *Languages in Contact. An Introductory Textbook on Translation / Manual introductorio a la traducción*. Lanham: University Press of America.

U.S. Department of Health and Human Sevices. "Your Rights under Title VI of the Civil Rights Act of 1964." http://www.hhs.gov/ocr/title6.html (accessed Nov. 20, 2006).

——. "Sus derechos bajo el Título VI del Acta de los Derechos Civiles de 1964." http://www.hhs.gov/ocr/factsheets/spanish/title6.html (accessed Nov. 20, 2006).

Vázquez Ayora, Gerardo. 1977. *Introducción a la traductología*. Washington, D.C.: Georgetown University Press.

Vennewitz, Leila. 1993. "Translator and Author: Some Relationships." In *The Art of Literary Translation*, Hans Schulte and Gerhart Teuscher, eds. Lanham: University Press of America, 85-102.

Venuti, Lawrence. 1995. *The Translator's Invisibility. A History of Translation*. London and New York: Routledge.

——. 1998. *The Scandals of Translation. Towards an Ethics of Difference*. London and New York: Routledge.

——. ed. 2003. *The Translation Studies Reader*. London and New York: Routledge.

Vinay, Jean Paul and Jean Darbelnet. 1958. *Stylistique compareé du français et de l'anglais*. Paris: Didier.

——. 1995. *Comparative Stylistics of French and English: A Methodology for Translation*. Trans. Juan C. Sager and M.J. Hamel, Amsterdam and Philadelphia: John Benjamins.

Whitley, M. Stanley. 2002. *Spanish/English Contrasts. A Course in Spanish Linguistics*. Washington D.C.: Georgetown University Press.

Williams, A. D. 1992. *Pope, Homer, and Manliness: Some Aspects of Eighteenth-Century Classical Learning*. London and New York, Routledge.

Wilss, Wolfram. 1993. "Translation Studies: The State of the Art." In *The Art of Literary Translation*, Hans Schulte and Gerhart Teuscher, eds. Lanham: University Press of America.

——. 2004. "Decision Making in Translation." In Mona Baker, ed., 57-60.

Yule, George. 1988. *The Study of Language*. Cambridge University Press.

——. 1998. *El lenguaje*. Trans. Nuria Bel Rafecas. Cambridge University Press.

Zaro, Juan Jesús and Michael Trumann. 1998. *Manual de Traducción / A Manual of Translation*. Madrid: SGEL.

INDEX

About the author

Lucía V. Aranda is Assistant Professor and Graduate Chair of Spanish at the University of Hawai'i at Manoa, where she teaches translation, Spanish, and U.S. Latino literature. She received her Ph.D. from the Universidad Completense in Madrid. Her research interests include translation studies, bilingualism, code-switching, second language acquisition and U.S. Latino literature.

Made in the USA
Columbia, SC
26 July 2021